ENGLISH PRONUNCIATION FOR INTERNATIONAL STUDENTS

ENGLISH PRONUNCIATION FOR INTERNATIONAL STUDENTS

PAULETTE WAINLESS DALE, Ph.D.

Miami-Dade Community College

LILLIAN POMS, M.Ed.

Hearing and Speech Center of Florida, Inc.

PRENTICE HALL REGENTS
Englewood Cliffs, New Jersey 07632

Library of Congress Cataloging-in-Publication Data

Dale, Paulette.
    English pronunciation for international students /
Paulette Dale, Lillian Poms.
        p.   cm.
    ISBN 0–13–279852–2
    1. English language—Textbooks for foreign speakers. 2. English language—
Pronunciation by foreign speakers. I. Poms, Lillian. II. Title.
PE1157.D35   1994
428.3′4—dc20   93–23687
                                                                            CIP

Printed on Recycled Paper

Acquisitions editor: Nancy Baxer
Editorial/production supervision: Peggy Gordon
Cover design: Yes Graphics
Production coordinator: Ray Keating

Prentice-Hall, Inc.
A Paramount Communications Company
Englewood Cliffs, New Jersey 07632

Printed in the United States of America
10   9   8   7   6   5   4   3

ISBN 0-13-279852-2

Prentice-Hall International (UK) Limited, *London*
Prentice-Hall of Australia Pty. Limited, *Sydney*
Prentice-Hall Canada Inc., *Toronto*
Prentice-Hall Hispanoamericana, S.A., *Mexico*
Prentice-Hall of India Private Limited, *New Delhi*
Prentice-Hall of Japan, Inc., *Tokyo*
Simon & Schuster Asia Pte. Ltd., *Singapore*
Editora Prentice-Hall do Brasil, Ltda., *Rio de Janeiro*

CONTENTS

SECTION II: VOWELS

SECTION III: STRESS, RHYTHM, AND INTONATION

APPENDIX I: TO THE TEACHER   *255*

APPENDIX II: ANSWERS   *273*

AUDIO CASSETTE TAPE OUTLINE

TAPE 1

Side A

Side A, *continued*

Side B

TAPE 2

TAPE 2, *continued*

INTRODUCTION

Welcome to **English Pronunciation for International Students**. Before we begin, we'd like to discuss "foreign accents" in general. Webster's Dictionary defines *accent* as "speech habits typical of the natives of a region." SO—we **all** have accents!

You should be PROUD of having an accent. In fact, there are advantages to having one. YES, we said advantages! A foreign accent tells listeners that you speak at least *TWO* languages. That certainly puts you far ahead of a person who can speak only one language. The world would be very dull if we all sounded the same. After all, *VARIETY IS THE SPICE OF LIFE!!!*

Unfortunately, there is a disadvantage to having a foreign accent. It may hinder effective communication in your non-native language and cause you to be misunderstood. Our main goal is to help you improve your pronunciation of American English. This will enable you to clearly communicate exactly what you want to say. We will be with you throughout this book to help you along the way!

Please turn the page and continue reading. The next section is not for *teachers*; it is ***especially for you!!!***

TO THE STUDENT

You bought **English Pronunciation for International Students** because you feel a need to improve your ability to speak English as a second language. We know it is frustrating to have someone say, "I can't understand you because of your accent." We also know that you might be afraid to use certain words because you'll mispronounce them. Many of our students avoid words like "rice" and "berry."

We understand your feelings and want to reassure you. PLEASE DON'T WORRY! You don't have to avoid saying certain words and phrases, and you don't have to be misunderstood by other people.

English Pronunciation for International Students has been written especially for YOU. You will find that this program has been designed to help you overcome your particular pronunciation problems with speaking English and that it is an independent program you can use **on your own**. The manual is written in easy-to-understand terms and is accompanied by cassette tapes to help you learn to pronounce American English sounds correctly. You don't need a teacher (or speech therapist) to use this program.

The **English Pronunciation for International Students** manual covers the various sounds in the English language. Each chapter follows a specific format and contains the following sections:

Pronouncing the Sound

A simple explanation of how to pronounce the sound and details for actual placement of the articulators (lips, tongue, etc.) are discussed.

Possible Pronunciation Problems

This section explains why the sound creates problems for you and the type of pronunciation difficulties you are likely to experience.

Hints

A series of rules to help you remember when to produce the sound are provided. They will help you use English spelling patterns as a guide to pronunciation.

Exercises

This section has a variety of exercises designed to give you comprehensive practice with the sound as it occurs in words, common phrases, and sentences.

Self-Tests

This section contains mini-tests to help you evaluate your progress. Your ability to recognize and pronounce the sound in words, sentences, and conversational activities will be tested.

For an Encore

This section is designed to give you practice in using the target sound in daily life. A variety of listening, reading, and conversational activities are provided at the end of each chapter.

Additional chapters include explanations and exercises for the use of English stress, rhythm, and intonation patterns, and the correct pronunciation of final consonants, past tense verbs, and plural nouns. Answers to all tests are given in Appendix II. The audio tapes that accompany the manual contain recorded sections of each chapter (a picture of a tape cassette next to an exercise tells you that the exercise is included on the tape). The tapes are designed to provide you with a model of correct pronunciation for each sound covered. Please refer to pages ix–xi for a complete outline of the material included on the cassette tapes.

USING THE *ENGLISH PRONUNCIATION FOR INTERNATIONAL STUDENTS* PROGRAM

Now you are ready to begin the program. The only other materials you will need are a cassette recorder to play the tapes and a mirror to help you correctly place your articulators to make the right sound. Find yourself a quiet, comfortable area to practice in; bring along your enthusiasm and determination to improve your speech—*and you're all ready to go!!!*

Before beginning the program, read the first chapter in the manual and play Tape 1 (Side A) completely to become familiar with the format of the lessons. (Be sure you understand the written explanations in the manual before beginning oral practice.)

Exercises

Rewind the tape to the beginning and look at Exercise A, page 12. Practice the exercise using the directions provided. Repeat the words after the instructor during the pauses. You can stop the tape whenever you like and repeat a section. If you have difficulty at any time, stop the tape and reread the directions for pronouncing the sound. Check in the mirror to be sure your articulators are in the correct position. Continue with each exercise until you feel you can say the words and sentences easily. Before starting the next section, you should be able to repeat the material after the instructor on the tape without looking at the book.

Self-Tests

After you are happy with your ability to do the exercises, begin the self-tests. The instructions for each self-test are different; read all the directions carefully before beginning. When you finish each test, turn off the recorder and check your answers in Appendix II. If you have any difficulty with the tests, return to the beginning of the chapter and repeat the exercises. The dialogues and paragraphs are the most difficult activities in each chapter; review them often as you progress through the manual.

For an Encore

When you're content with your pronunciation of the target sound in the exercises and self-tests, you are ready to progress from the book to "real life" situations. "For an Encore" provides a few suggestions to guide you in making your correct pronunciation of the sound automatic. Try to find other ways to incorporate the sound into your daily routine.

Review Roundups

Review chapters are designed to give you additional practice. Complete the tests as you did in the previous chapters. If you have difficulty with one of the sounds, return to the appropriate chapter and review.

Practice Sessions

It is very important to practice as much as possible. Try to follow a definite time schedule. Daily practice sessions are ideal, but if your time is limited, try to practice at least three or four times a week (even if only for 20 to 30 minutes). **We know that reading the book and listening to the tapes is VERY hard work. TAKE A BREAK WHEN YOU GET TIRED.** Continue your study session when you feel refreshed. DON'T TRY TO DO IT ALL AT ONCE! **Improvement takes time. BUT, little by little, you will succeed!**

Keep your tape recorder and cassettes handy to use in the kitchen while you are preparing dinner or in the car while you're driving to work. Practice when you're relaxed, rested, and motivated so you will do your very best. **PRACTICE MAKES PERFECT!!!**

OTHER WAYS TO IMPROVE YOUR SPEECH

LISTENING to correct pronunciation patterns is as important as practicing them. Take advantage of as many opportunities as possible to hear English being spoken correctly. You can do this by following these suggestions:

1. Watch the evening news on TV. Pay careful attention to the newscaster's pronunciation of words. Repeat some of these words and phrases out loud. *(Your family won't think you are talking to yourself—they'll admire you for trying to improve!)*
2. Listen to radio news stations for 5 to 10 minutes at a time. Repeat common words and phrases after the announcer. *(If anyone gives you a strange look, just tell the person you are practicing your speech!)*
3. When one of your favorite TV shows is on, try to understand the dialogue without watching. *OR*, if you must keep your eyes glued to the screen every minute, wait for the commercials to practice your listening skills without watching.
4. Converse frequently with native American English speakers.
5. Ask your listener if you are pronouncing a specific word correctly. *He or she will be glad to help!*
6. **Most important of all—BE BRAVE!** The exercises are full of common expressions. Use some of them in real conversations. For example, *See you this evening* or *Pleased to meet you* are common phrases you can easily practice. No one will realize that you are doing your homework!!!

Although this program emphasizes pronunciation, the material used in the manual can help you increase your vocabulary also. When you don't understand a word or idiom, look it up in the dictionary. Write the definition in your manual so you won't forget it.

You might be wondering how long it will take before you actually see some improvement in your speech. We believe that **English Pronunciation for International Students** provides you with everything you need to improve your speech. If you follow the program as it is outlined, you should notice an improvement in just a few weeks. *Remember—THE MORE YOU PRACTICE, THE FASTER YOU WILL IMPROVE!*

Motivation really can contribute to changes in speech. Many aspiring actors and actresses have lost heavy accents in order to become movie stars. We can't guarantee you a movie contract, but we know that following this program will help you to be better understood and to communicate better in your everyday lives. **Good luck!**

TURN THE PAGE AND LET'S GET STARTED!!

A KEY TO PRONOUNCING
THE CONSONANTS
OF AMERICAN ENGLISH

You have probably discovered that there is a big difference between the way words are spelled in English and how they are pronounced. English spelling patterns are inconsistent and are not always a reliable guide to pronunciation. For example, in the following words, the letters *ch* are used to represent **three** different sounds.

*ma**ch**ine   **ch**ain   me**ch**anic*

Pretty confusing, right? That's why we need a set of symbols in which **each** sound is represented by a **different** symbol. In this program, you will learn the International Phonetic Alphabet (IPA), which is used all over the world. It consists of a set of symbols in which **one symbol** always represents **one sound**.

Many modern dictionaries use the IPA in addition to a system of symbols known as *diacritical marks* to help you pronounce words. Since you frequently refer to a dictionary when reading and speaking English, we have included the most common dictionary equivalents of the IPA symbols.

DON'T WORRY! It won't be necessary to learn all the symbols at once. Each consonant will be introduced and explained **one at a time**. You will learn the symbols easily as you progress through the book. A pronunciation key of the different consonants of American English with their IPA and dictionary symbols is presented on page 10. Refer to it often for a quick review.

To help you learn the exact pronunciation of the phonetic symbols and key words, the **Key to Pronouncing the Consonants of American English** on the next page has been recorded at the beginning of Tape 1, Side A. Each phonetic symbol will be pronounced and each English key word will be said once. Listen carefully to this first recording **before** continuing with the program.

DEFINITIONS

As you progress through this manual, you will frequently see the terms **gum ridge, soft palate, aspiration, voiced consonant, voiceless consonant,** and **articulators**. We will now define these terms for you.

GUM RIDGE: The gum ridge is the hard part of the roof of your mouth, just behind your upper front teeth.

SOFT PALATE: The soft palate is the soft, movable, rear portion of the roof of your mouth.

ASPIRATION: Aspiration means the action of pronouncing a sound with a puff of released breath. Certain consonants in English ([p], [t], [k], and [h]) are "aspirate" sounds. They should be produced with a strong puff of air.

VOICED CONSONANT: A voiced consonant is a sound produced when the vocal cords are vibrating. Place your hand on your throat over your vocal cords while making a humming sound. You can feel your vocal cords vibrate as you say "*mmmmmmmmm.*"

VOICELESS CONSONANT: A voiceless consonant is a sound made with no vibration of the vocal cords. Put your hand over your vocal cords and make the hissing sound "*sssssssss.*" You will *not* feel any vibration this time!

ARTICULATORS: The articulators are the different parts of the mouth area that we use when speaking, such as the lips, tongue, soft palate, teeth, and jaw.

The various consonant sounds are created by:

1. **The position of your articulators.** For example, the tip of your tongue must touch the upper gum ridge to say sounds like [t], [d], [n], or [l], but must protrude between your teeth to say [θ] as in *think* or [ð] as in *them.*
2. **The way the airstream comes from your mouth or nose.** For example, the air or breath stream is continuous for the consonants [s] or [f], but is completely stopped and then exploded for [p] or [t]. The airstream flows through the *nose* for [m], [n], and [ŋ] and through the *mouth* for all other consonants.
3. **The vibration of your vocal cords.** For example, your vocal cords do *not* vibrate for the sounds [s], [f], or [t], but you must add "voicing" for sounds [z], [v], or [d].

The chart on page 9 categorizes the voiced and voiceless consonants. Don't try to memorize the chart! Put your hand over your vocal cords as you say the following sounds. You will be able to hear and **"feel"** the difference between voiced and voiceless consonants.

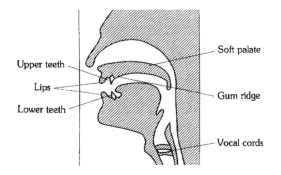

VOICED	VOICELESS
[b]	[p]
[d]	[t]
[g]	[k]
[v]	[f]
[z]	[s]
[ð]	[θ]
[dʒ]	[tʃ]
[ʒ]	[ʃ]
[m], [n], [ŋ]	[h]
[j], [w], [l], [r]	

A KEY TO PRONOUNCING THE CONSONANTS OF AMERICAN ENGLISH

International Phonetic Alphabet Symbol	Dictionary Symbol	English Key Words
[s]	s	sit, basket, kiss
[z]	z	zoo, busy, buzz
[t]	t	top, return, cat
[d]	d	day, ladder, bed
[θ]	th	think, bathtub, mouth
[ð]	*th*	the, father, smooth
[ʃ]	sh	shoe, nation, wish
[tʃ]	ch	chair, witch
[ʒ]	zh	rouge, vision, measure
[dʒ]	j	jaw, magic, age
[j]	y	you, yes
[p]	p	pay, apple, stop
[b]	b	boy, rabbit, tub
[f]	f	fun, office, if
[v]	v	very, over, save
[k]	k	cake, car, book
[g]	g	go, begin, egg
[w]	w	we, away
[l]	l	lamp, pillow, bell
[r]	r	red, marry, car
[h]	h	hat, behind
[m]	m	me, swim
[n]	n	no, run
[ŋ]	ŋ	sing, playing

[l] as in *LAMP, YELLOW,* and *POOL*
(DICTIONARY MARK: l)
and
[r] as in *RED, MARRY,* and *FAR*
(DICTIONARY MARK: r)

PRONOUNCING [l]

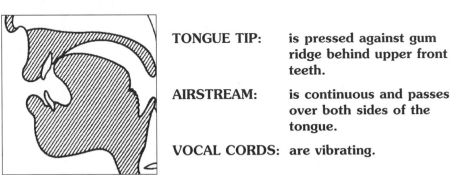

TONGUE TIP:	**is pressed against gum ridge behind upper front teeth.**
AIRSTREAM:	**is continuous and passes over both sides of the tongue.**
VOCAL CORDS:	**are vibrating.**

POSSIBLE PRONUNCIATION PROBLEMS

The consonant [l] may not exist in your language. The differences between English [l] and [r] may be difficult for you to hear, causing you to confuse the two sounds.

EXAMPLES: If you substitute [r] for [l]: **flight** becomes **fright**.
                            late becomes **rate**.

The consonant [l] will be easier for you to say if you concentrate on feeling your tongue tip press against your upper gum ridge like [t]. *Learn your lessons well. You will say a perfect* [l]*!*

 **EXERCISE A**

The following words should be pronounced with [l]. Repeat them after your teacher or the instructor on the tape. (Be sure your tongue tip touches your upper gum ridge.)

[l] At the Beginning

let	long
leg	light
live	leave
late	listen
last	little

[l] In the Middle

only	collect
alive	family
hello	yellow
salad	believe
alone	balloon

 EXERCISE B

When [l] is the last sound in a word, the back of the tongue should be raised higher than for [l] at the beginning or in the middle of words. Repeat the following words after your teacher or the instructor on the tape. **Be sure to raise the back of your tongue higher in the mouth toward the soft palate.**

[l] At the End

all	able
tell	apple
fill	table
call	people
fool	trouble

EXERCISE C

When speaking English, speakers of other languages frequently produce consonant blends incorrectly by inserting a vowel between sounds (for example, **plight** becomes **polite**). Read the following words aloud. Be sure **NOT** to insert a vowel before the [l] in each word. **This exercise is not on the tape.**

1. **bl**ack
2. **bl**end
3. **gl**ow
4. **pl**ease
5. **cl**oud
6. **bl**ock
7. **fl**ag
8. dis**pl**ay
9. a**fl**oat
10. **sl**ide

EXERCISE D

The boldface words in the following phrases and sentences should be pronounced with [l]. Read them as accurately as possible. **This exercise is not on the tape.**

1. **telephone call**
2. **Leave** me **alone**.
3. **lots** of **luck**
4. **Light** the **candle**.
5. **Please believe** me.
6. **Learn** your **lesson**.
7. **Will** you **mail** the **letter**?
8. The **little girl fell asleep**.
9. **Lucy lost** her **locket**.
10. He who **laughs last, laughs** best.
11. Do you **like chocolate** or **vanilla**?
12. The **airplane flight leaves** at **eleven**.
13. His **family lives** in **Maryland**.
14. You can't **fool all** of the **people all** of the time.
15. **Leave** the **umbrella** in the **hall closet**.

 **SELF-TEST I**   (Correct answers may be found in Appendix II on p. 273.)

Listen carefully to your teacher or the instructor on the tape as the following pairs of words are presented. **ONE** word in each pair contains [l]. Circle the number of the word with the consonant [l].

EXAMPLE: The instructor says: **lane**   **rain**
                      You circle: ①   2

1. 1   2
2. 1   2
3. 1   2
4. 1   2
5. 1   2

《**LEARN YOUR LESSONS WELL. YOU WILL SAY A PERFECT** [l]**!**》

PRONOUNCING [r]

TONGUE TIP:	**is curled upward but does NOT touch the roof of the mouth.**
AIRSTREAM:	**is continuous.**
VOCAL CORDS:	**are vibrating.**

POSSIBLE PRONUNCIATION PROBLEMS

The sound [r] as it is pronounced in English may not exist in your language. The [r] in many languages is a blend of English [r] and [l] and is produced by rapidly touching your tongue tip to the roof of your mouth. Your pronunciation problems occur when you attempt to say the English [r] by touching the roof of your mouth with your tongue. This results in the substitution of [l].

EXAMPLES: If you say [l] instead of [r]:   **berry** becomes **belly**.
  rice   becomes **lice**.

Never allow your tongue tip to touch your upper gum ridge. **Remember to p̲ractice [r] ca̲refully. Your̲ [r] will be R̲IGHT on TA̲R̲GET!**

EXERCISE A

The following words should be pronounced with [r]. Repeat them carefully after your teacher or the instructor on the tape. *Be sure your tongue does NOT touch your upper gum ridge when you say* [r].

[r] At the Beginning	[r] In the Middle	[r] At the End
red	very	or
run	marry	are
row	story	far
read	berry	door
rest	sorry	near
rich	hurry	more
rain	carrot	sure
real	orange	their
wrong	around	before
write	tomorrow	appear

EXERCISE B

As with [l]-blends, you may produce [r]-blends incorrectly by inserting a vowel sound before the [r] (**bride** becomes "**buride**"). Read the following words aloud. Be careful not to insert a vowel before the [r] in each word. **This exercise is not on the tape.**

1. bring
2. cry
3. tree
4. proud
5. drink
6. freeze
7. grow
8. press
9. broke
10. dry

EXERCISE C

The boldface words in the following phrases and sentences should be pronounced with [r]. Repeat them carefully after your teacher or the instructor on the tape.

1. **Where are** you?
2. **near or far**
3. **Are** you **sure**?
4. See you **tomorrow**.
5. I'm **very sorry**.
6. He'll be **right there**.
7. **Roy returns tomorrow morning**.
8. The **train arrives every hour**.
9. I **already read** that **short story**.
10. **Rose** is **wearing** a **red dress**.
11. **Robert ran around** the **corner**.
12. **Rita** and **Larry are married**.
13. **Remember, never** put the **cart before** the **horse**!
14. **Mark** couldn't **start** the **car**.
15. I **rented** a **four-room** apartment.

SELF-TEST I   (Correct answers may be found in Appendix II on p. 273.)

The first word in each of the following pairs begins with the sound [r]. Write a letter in the blank before the second word to form a new [r]-consonant-blend word. **This self-test is not on the tape.**

EXAMPLE: ride   <u>b</u>ride

1. read   _ read
2. right   _ right
3. rip   _ rip
4. ream   _ ream
5. row   _ row
6. rain   _ rain
7. rash   _ rash
8. room   _ room
9. round   _ round
10. race   _ race

After checking your answers in Appendix II, practice reading these pairs of words aloud.

《**REMEMBER TO PRACTICE [r] CAREFULLY.**

YOUR [r] WILL BE RIGHT ON TARGET!》

Contrast and Review
of [l] and [r]

🔲 **ORAL EXERCISE I**

Repeat the pairs of words and sentences carefully after your teacher or the instructor on the tape. **Be sure your tongue touches the gum ridge for** [l] **but NOT for** [r].

[l]	**[r]**
1. late	rate
2. led	red
3. low	row
4. elect	erect
5. believe	bereave

6. Move toward the **light**.   Move toward the **right**.
7. Can you **collect** the papers?   Can you **correct** the papers?
8. Is there a **lack** of lamb?   Is there a **rack** of lamb?
9. It was very **long**.   It was very **wrong**.
10. Please remove the **lock**.   Please remove the **rock**.

11. Carry that **load** down the **road**.
       [l]   [r]
12. We saw a **palace** in **Paris**.
         [l]   [r]
13. I left the **rake** near the **lake**.
      [r]   [l]
14. He **lied** about the long **ride**.
   [l]   [r]
15. **Jerry** likes **jelly** and bread.
   [r]   [l]

ORAL EXERCISE II

Read each of the following consonant blend pairs aloud. Remember to produce the two consonants at the beginning of each word smoothly and without inserting a vowel between. Example: bloom–broom **NOT** balum–barum.
This exercise is not on the tape.

[l]	[r]
1. play	pray
2. clue	crew
3. glow	grow
4. flock	frock
5. clash	crash

6. We had a **fright** on that **flight**.
          [r]   [l]
7. That **brand** of food is **bland**.
    [r]   [l]
8. Did **Blake break** his leg?
    [l]   [r]
9. The **crew** had no **clue** of the storm.
    [r]   [l]
10. **Fred fled** from the room.
   [r]   [l]

REVIEW TEST I   (Correct answers may be found in Appendix II on p. 273.)

Listen carefully to your teacher or to the instructor on the tape as ten three-word series are presented. Two of the words in each group will be the **SAME**; one will be **DIFFERENT**. Circle the number of the word that is **different**.

EXAMPLE: The instructor says: law   law   raw
                     You circle: 1   2   ③

1.	1 2 3		6.	1 2 3
2.	1 2 3		7.	1 2 3
3.	1 2 3		8.	1 2 3
4.	1 2 3		9.	1 2 3
5.	1 2 3		10.	1 2 3

(Correct answers may be found in Appendix II on p. 274.)

Your teacher or the instructor on the tape will present the following sentences using ONLY ONE of the choices. Listen carefully and circle the word (and consonant) used.

EXAMPLE:	We all really like	(plays	praise).
		[l]	[r]

1. Don't step on the (glass grass).
   [l] [r]

2. Please put this on your (list wrist).
   [l] [r]

3. The whole family was (pleasant present).
   [l] [r]

4. It was a horrid (climb crime).
   [l] [r]

5. Look at the bright red (flame frame).
   [l] [r]

After checking your answers in Appendix II, read each of the sentences twice. Use the first word in the first reading and the contrast word in the second reading.

REVIEW TEST III

(Correct answers may be found in Appendix II on p. 274.)

Listen carefully to your teacher or to the tape as five sentences are presented. One word in each sentence will be said INCORRECTLY. On the line to the right of each number write the CORRECT word.

	Correct Word	Sentence
EXAMPLE A:	right	(Make a light turn at the corner.)
EXAMPLE B:	belly	(He had a berry ache.)

1. _____

2. _____

3. _____

4. _____

5. _____

FOR AN ENCORE . . . .

READING

Look in the classified section of the newspaper. Circle all words pronounced with [l] and underline all [r] words in a least three ads. Read them aloud.

CONVERSATION

The colors of the rainbow are filled with [l] and [r] consonant sounds (yellow, blue, green, orange, red, etc.). Every time you mention color in conversation, remember to use your [r] and [l] sounds correctly!

《**REMEMBER TO PRACTICE AND LEARN** [r] **AND** [l] **WELL!**》

[s] as in *SIT, BASKET,* and *KISS*
(DICTIONARY MARK: s)

PRONOUNCING [s]

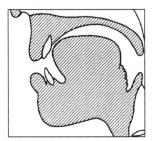

TIP OF TONGUE: is near but does not touch gum ridge behind upper front teeth.*

AIRSTREAM: is continuous without interruption.

VOCAL CORDS: are not vibrating.

POSSIBLE PRONUNCIATION PROBLEMS

The sound [s] is a common sound and should be easy for you to say. However, many speakers tend to say [ʃ] instead of [s] before [i] and [ɪ].

EXAMPLES: If you say [ʃ] instead of [s]:   **see** will sound like **she**.
sip will sound like **ship**.

As you say [s] keep the airstream steady, like the hissing sound of a snake (sssssssss)! *So study and practice; you'll soon have success with* [s]*!*

---

*Some speakers produce [s] more easily by placing the tip of the tongue behind the lower teeth.

EXERCISE A

The following words should be pronounced with [s]. Repeat them after your teacher or the instructor on the tape. (Be sure you say [s] and not [ʃ].)

[s] At the Beginning	[s] In the Middle	[s] At the End
seat	bicycle	bus
seek	missing	yes
city	accident	box
sick	exceed	miss
seen	consider	face

[s] Spelled:

"s"	"c"	"x" ([ks])	"ss"
system	cinema	six	kiss
sink	citizen	fix	less
desk	concede	fox	dresser
must	cedar	tax	message
wasp	icing	oxen	

Less frequent spelling patterns for [s] consist of the letters *z* and *sc*.

EXAMPLES: waltz pretzel scent scene

> **HINTS:** 1. The letter *s* is the most common spelling pattern for [s].
>
> 2. The letter *c* followed by *e*, *i*, or *y* is usually pronounced [s].
>
> EXAMPLES: cent place society fancy
>
> 3. The letter *s* in plural nouns is pronounced [s] when it follows most voiceless consonants.
>
> EXAMPLES: books coats cuffs maps

EXERCISE B

The boldface words in the phrases and sentences should be pronounced with [s]. Read them aloud as accurately as possible. (Avoid using the [ʃ] sound.) **This exercise is not on the tape.**

1. **sink** or **swim**
2. **sing** a **song**
3. **east** and **west**
4. it **seems** to me
5. **smoke** a **cigar**
6. **simmer** the **soup**
7. **Sid has seven sisters.**
8. The **sea seems smooth.**
9. **Cindy was seen** in the **city.**
10. **Sixteen minus six** is ten.

 ## SELF-TEST I   (Correct answers may be found in Appendix II on p. 274.)

Listen carefully to your teacher or to the instructor on the tape as the following five words are presented. Some of them will be deliberately mispronounced. Circle **C** for **"Correct"** or **I** for **"Incorrect"** to indicate if the word was pronounced correctly or incorrectly.

EXAMPLE A: **sift**   C   (I)   (The instructor says "**shift**.")
EXAMPLE B: **seek**   (C)   I   (The instructor says "**seek**.")

1. sin   C   I
2. sip   C   I
3. simmer   C   I
4. single   C   I
5. seize   C   I

FOR AN ENCORE . . . .

READING

Read several advertisements in your local newspaper. Underline all words pronounced with [s]. Practice reading the ad aloud. Be sure to pronounce the [s] words correctly.

⟨⟨**REMEMBER TO <u>S</u>TUDY AND YOU'LL**

<u>S</u>OON HAVE <u>S</u>UC<u>C</u>E<u>SS</u> WITH [s]**!**⟩⟩

[z] as in *ZOO, BUSY,* and *BUZZ*
(DICTIONARY MARK: z)

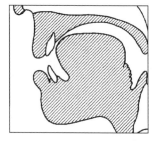

TONGUE: is in the same position as for [s].

AIRSTREAM: is continuous without interruption.

VOCAL CORDS: are vibrating.

POSSIBLE PRONUNCIATION PROBLEMS

The sound [z] is not a common sound. You probably pronounce the letter *z* in English as an [s] or a [dʒ]. Also, irregular English spelling patterns contribute to your problems with this consonant.

EXAMPLE A: If you say [s] instead of [z]: **zoo** will sound like **Sue**.
EXAMPLE B: If you say [dʒ] instead of [z]: **zest** will sound like **jest**.

Remember, [z] is a voiced sound; your vocal cords **MUST** vibrate or you will say [s] by mistake. *Think of the buzzing sound of a bee (bZZZZZZZZZZZZZZZZZZZZZZ) and you'll say your Z's with EASE!*

 **EXERCISE A**

The following words should be pronounced with [z]. Repeat them after your teacher or the instructor on the tape. (Be sure to add voice by making your vocal cords vibrate.)

[z] At the Beginning	[z] In the Middle	[z] At the End
zoo	lazy	as
zeal	busy	is
zebra	easy	his
zero	crazy	was
zipper	dozen	buzz

[z] Spelled:

"z"	"s"
zip	has
size	eyes
seize	rose
lizard	these
sneeze	bruise

The letter *x* is a less common spelling pattern for [z].

EXAMPLES: xylophone   xerox

> **HINTS:** 1. The letter z is usually pronounced [z].
>
>   EXAMPLES: zipper cozy freeze
>
> 2. The letter s is usually pronounced [z] when between vowels in a stressed syllable.
>
>   EXAMPLES: desérve becáuse resígn presént
>
> 3. The letter s in plural nouns is pronounced [z] when it follows a vowel or most voiced consonants.
>
>   EXAMPLES: shoes legs leaves beds cars

> **NOTE:** The vowel BEFORE [z] at the end of a word is always pro-
> longed more than before [s]. Prolonging the vowel before
> [z] helps to distinguish it from [s].*
>
> EXAMPLES eye<u>s</u> bree<u>z</u>e ri<u>s</u>e bu<u>zz</u>

EXERCISE B

Repeat the following pairs of words after your teacher or the instructor on the tape. **REMEMBER** [z] is a voiced sound; your vocal cords should vibrate. (Be sure to prolong any sound **BEFORE** the sound [z].)

[s]	[z]
Sue	zoo
face	phase
race	raise
bus	buzz
ice	eyes

EXERCISE C

The boldface words in the following phrases and sentences should be pro-nounced with [z]. Repeat them carefully after your teacher or the instructor on the tape. (Remember to add voicing when saying words with [z].)

1. **Easy does** it.
2. **zero degrees**
3. a cool **breeze**
4. a **dozen eggs**
5. **busy as** a bee
6. **Close** your **eyes.**
7. The **puzzle is easy.**
8. I **raise flowers.**
9. There are **zebras** and **lions** at the **zoo.**
10. **His cousin comes** from New **Zealand.**

*The same rule applies to the voiced consonants [b], [d], [v], and [g]. (See appropriate chapters.)

SELF-TEST I   (Correct answers may be found in Appendix II on p. 274.)

Repeat the following words after your teacher or the instructor on the tape. Circle the letter *s* in each word that is pronounced [z]. (Only ONE *s* in each word is actually pronounced [z].)

EXAMPLE: s u r p r i ⓢ e

1. s u p p o s e
2. S u s a n
3. d i s a s t e r
4. e a s i e s t
5. t i s s u e s

FOR AN ENCORE . . . .

CONVERSATION

Every time you mention the days of the week Tue_s_day, Wedne_s_day, or Thur_s_day, be sure to pronounce the [z] sounds correctly.

《REVIEW THIS CHAPTER OFTEN AND YOU'LL
SAY YOUR Z'S WITH EA_S_E!》

[t] as in *TOP, RETURN,* and *CAT*
(DICTIONARY MARK: t)

PRONOUNCING [t]

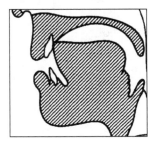

TONGUE TIP: is firmly pressed against gum ridge behind upper front teeth.

AIRSTREAM: is stopped and then exploded.

VOCAL CORDS: are not vibrating.

POSSIBLE PRONUNCIATION PROBLEMS

The sound [t] is a common sound and easy for you to say. However, many speakers tend to say [ts] instead of [t] before [u], or [tʃ] in place of [t] before [i] and [ɪ].

EXAMPLE A: If you say [ts] instead of [t]: **two** will sound like **tsu.**

                                                       tune will sound like **tsune.**

EXAMPLE B: If you say [tʃ] instead of [t]: **tease** will sound like **cheese.**

                                                       tin   will sound like **chin.**

*Jus*t *be sure* t*o prac*t*ice all the* t*ime. Your* [t] *will be* t*errific!*

> **NOTE:** Many speakers tend to add the sound [o] to words ending in [t] in English (*cuto, sito, cato*). Be sure you avoid this extra vowel when practicing words with final [t].

EXERCISE A

Read the following [t] words aloud. Be sure that [ts], [tʃ] or [o] are not inserted by mistake. **This exercise is not on the tape.**

[t] At the Beginning	[t] In the Middle	[t] At the End
to/two/too	attic	it
tube	until	but
took	attend	boat
tea	notice	late
team	romantic	light
		feet

 # EXERCISE B

The boldface words in the following phrases and sentences should be pronounced with [t]. Repeat them carefully after your teacher or the instructor on the tape. **Guard against** [ts], [tʃ] **and adding** [o]!

1. **Tell** the **teacher.**
2. **tea** and **toast**
3. **to** be or **not to** be
4. **light** on your **feet**
5. **Today** is **Tuesday**.
6. **That team** is the **top** winner.
7. **Tim bought two tickets**.
8. **Pat wrote** the **letter**.
9. The **boat won't return until eight.**
10. Leave the **waiter** a **fifteen percent tip.**

SELF-TEST I   (Correct answers may be found in Appendix II on p. 275.)

Read the following sentences aloud. Circle the [t]-word that correctly completes the sentence. **This self-test is not on the tape.**

1. (two too)   Tess had _____ much to eat.
2. (two too)   I must return _____ TVs.
3. (right write) "Two wrongs don't make a _____."
4. (right write) Please _____ me a note.
5. (aunt ant)   Tim's _____ is twenty-two.

HINTS: 1. The letter *t* is usually pronounced [t].

2. The letters *ed* in past tense verbs are pronounced [t] when they follow a voiceless consonant.

EXAMPLES: stopp*ed*   look*ed*   kiss*ed*   wash*ed*

SELF-TEST II   (Correct answers may be found in Appendix II on p. 275.)

Read the following dialogue aloud with a friend. Circle all words pronounced with [t]. **This self-test is not on the tape.**

•••

TIM: Tina, who were you talking to on the telephone?

TINA: Terry White. She wanted to know what time the party is tonight.

TIM: Terry is always late. She missed our tennis game last Tuesday.

TINA: Two days ago, she didn't come to breakfast until two. Terry is always in a tizzy!

TIM: Terry missed her flight to Tucson last week.

TINA: That routine of hers is typical!

TIM: This is terrible! What time did you tell her to come tonight?

TINA: I told Terry to come at six fifteen. The party is really at eight!

TIM: To tell the truth, I wish you told her it was at two. I don't trust her!

•••

FOR AN ENCORE . . . .

CONVERSATION

Use the following common [t] phrases when talking to different people at home, school, or work. *What time is it? Take your time. What is your telephone number?*

⟨⟨**EVERY TIME YOU TALK, TRY TO SAY A PERFECT** [t]**.**⟩⟩

[d] as in *DAY*, *LADDER*, and *BED*
(DICTIONARY MARK: d)

PRONOUNCING [d]

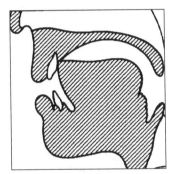

TIP OF TONGUE: is firmly pressed against gum ridge behind upper front teeth.

AIRSTREAM: is stopped and then exploded.

VOCAL CORDS: are vibrating.

POSSIBLE PRONUNCIATION PROBLEMS

1. The sound [d] should be produced with the tip of your tongue touching the upper gum ridge and **NOT** the back of your upper front teeth.
2. When [d] is the last sound in a word, many speakers forget to make their vocal cords vibrate. This will make [d] sound like a [t] and confuse your listeners.

EXAMPLES: If you say [t] instead of [d]:   **card** will sound like **cart**.
bed will sound like **bet**.

Your [d] will be perfect if you press the tip of your tongue against the gum ridge behind your upper front teeth *and* add voicing. ___Don't forget to practice__ [d] *every __day__!*

EXERCISE A

The following words should be pronounced with [d]. Repeat them after your teacher or the instructor on the tape. (Be sure your tongue tip touches the upper gum ridge.)

[d] At the Beginning	[d] In the Middle	[d] At the End
do	body	bad
dog	soda	did
day	today	end
desk	window	said
dime	pudding	food

EXERCISE B

Read the following pairs of words aloud. Be sure to press your tongue tip against the upper gum ridge and to make your vocal cords vibrate for [d]. (Remember to prolong any vowel BEFORE the consonant [d]. **This exercise is not on the tape.**

[d]	[t]
bed	bet
mad	mat
need	neat
hide	height
wade	wait

EXERCISE C

Read the following phrases and sentences aloud. The boldface words should be pronounced with [d]. **This exercise is not on the tape.**

1. a **good idea**
2. one **hundred dollars**
3. **end** of the **road**
4. a **bad cold**
5. What's **today's date?**
6. How **do** you **do?**
7. What **did** you **order** for **dinner?**
8. **Wendy** is a **wonderful dancer.**
9. The **dog** is **hiding under** the **bed.**
10. **Send dad** a **birthday card.**

SELF-TEST I   (Correct answers may be found in Appendix II on p. 275.)

Read the following wedding invitation aloud. Circle all words pronounced with [d]. **This self-test is not on the tape.**

Mr. and Mrs. Ed Dean
cordially invite you
to the wedding of their daughter
WENDY DEAN
to
DAN DEWEY
on Sunday, the twenty-third of December,
at the Diner's Club
1020 Davis Road, Dodge, North Dakota

RECEPTION AND DINNER FOLLOWING WEDDING
RSVP by Wednesday, December third

FOR AN ENCORE ....

CONVERSATION

Start a conversation with such expressions as *"Today's a nice day, isn't it?"* or *"What's today's date; I don't remember?"*

《**DON'T FORGET TO PRACTICE** [d] **EVERY DAY!**》

[θ] as in *THINK, BATHTUB,* and *MOUTH*
(DICTIONARY MARK: th)

PRONOUNCING [θ]

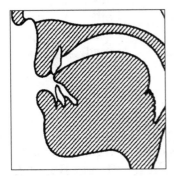

TONGUE TIP:	**is placed between the teeth.**
AIRSTREAM:	**is continuous without interruption.**
VOCAL CORDS:	**are not vibrating.**

POSSIBLE PRONUNCIATION PROBLEMS

The sound [θ] does not exist in most languages. Because it may be difficult to recognize, international students substitute a variety of more familiar sounds.

EXAMPLES: If you substitute [s] for [θ]:   **thank** will sound like **sank**.
   If you substitute [ʃ] for [θ]:   **thin**   will sound like **shin**.

   If you substitute [f] for [θ]:   **Ruth**   will sound like **roof**.
   If you substitute [t] for [θ]:   **path**   will sound like **pat**.

The sound [θ] will be easy for you to pronounce if you CONCENTRATE on placing your tongue between your teeth (LOOK IN A MIRROR), and keep the airstream continuous. ***Keep <u>thinking</u> about*** [θ].

EXERCISE A

The following words should be pronounced with [θ]. Repeat them after your teacher or the instructor on the tape. (Remember to place your tongue between your teeth.)

[θ] At the Beginning	[θ] In the Middle	[θ] At the End
thaw	author	path
thin	nothing	bath
thank	something	both
thief	anything	cloth
theme	method	mouth

EXERCISE B

Repeat the following rows of words after your teacher or the instructor on the tape. Place your tongue **BETWEEN** your teeth for [θ] and **BEHIND** your teeth for [t] and [s].

[θ]	[s]	[t]
thank	sank	tank
thin	sin	tin
thick	sick	tick
bath	bass	bat
Beth	Bess	bet

EXERCISE C

The boldface words in the following phrases and sentences should be pronounced with the consonant [θ]. Repeat them carefully after your teacher or the instructor on the tape.

1. **Thank** you.
2. I **think** so.
3. **something** else
4. Open your **mouth.**
5. **healthy** and **wealthy**
6. penny for your **thoughts**
7. **Thanksgiving** falls on **Thursday.**
8. Do birds fly **north** or **south** in the winter?
9. **Thank** you for your **thoughtful birthday** card.
10. The baby got his **third tooth** this **month.**

SELF-TEST I   (Correct answers may be found in Appendix II on p. 276.)

Read the following paragraph about **_Jim Thorpe_** aloud. Circle all words that should be pronounced with the consonant [θ]. **This self-test is not on the tape.**

∙∙

Do you know (anything) about Jim (Thorpe?) He was an American Indian athlete. He excelled in everything at the Olympics. Thousands were angry when Thorpe's medals were taken away because he was called a professional athlete. In 1973, long after his death, Thorpe's medals were restored. Throughout the world, Jim Thorpe is thought to be one of the greatest male athletes.

∙∙

After checking your answers in Appendix II, practice reading the paragraph again. Be sure to place your tongue BETWEEN your teeth as you say [θ].

FOR AN ENCORE ....

CONVERSATION

No one ever tires of hearing ***Thank you!*** Each time you say *thank you* to someone, be sure to pronounce the [θ] correctly.

〈〈KEEP **THINKING** ABOUT [θ]!〉〉

[ð] as in *THE, FATHER,* and *SMOOTH*
(DICTIONARY MARK: *th*)

PRONOUNCING [ð]

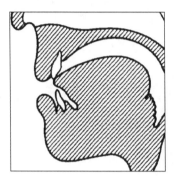

TIP OF TONGUE: is placed between the teeth.

AIRSTREAM: is continuous without interruption.

VOCAL CORDS: are vibrating.

POSSIBLE PRONUNCIATION PROBLEMS

The sound [ð] is another unfamiliar sound. It may be difficult for you to recognize and produce. You probably substitute the more familiar sound [d] or possibly [z] or [dʒ].

EXAMPLES: If you substitute [d]   for [ð]: **they**   will sound like **day.**
If you substitute [z]   for [ð]: **bathe** will sound like **bays.**
If you substitute [dʒ] for [ð]: **those** will sound like **Joe's.**

When pronouncing [ð], remember to place your tongue between your teeth and to keep the airstream from your mouth continuous. **LOOK IN THE MIRROR as you practice the [ð] exercises. *Make sure you can SEE the tip of your tongue, and such words as* <u>th</u>ese, <u>th</u>em, *and* <u>th</u>ose *will be pronounced perfectly!***

EXERCISE A

The following words should be pronounced with [ð]. Repeat them after your teacher or the instructor on the tape. (Be sure that your vocal cords are vibrating **AND** that your tongue is between your teeth.)

[ð] At the Beginning	[ð] In the Middle	[ð] At the End
the	other	bathe
this	mother	clothe
then	father	smooth
them	brother	breathe
that	gather	soothe

> **HINT:** The letters *th* followed by *e* are usually pronounced [ð].
>
> EXAMPLES: the them other bathe

EXERCISE B

Repeat the following rows of words after your teacher or the instructor on the tape. Place your tongue **BETWEEN** your teeth for [ð] and **BEHIND** your teeth for [d] and [z].

[ð]	[z]	[d]
then	Zen	den
breathe	breeze	breed
soothe	sues	sued
bathe	bays	bade
writhe	rise	ride

EXERCISE C

The boldface words in the following phrases and sentences should be pronounced with the consonant [ð]. Repeat them carefully after your teacher or the instructor on the tape.

1. **That's** right.
2. **father** and **mother**
3. **either** one of **them**
4. **This** is it!
5. wet **weather**
6. Don't **bother** me!
7. **This** is my **other brother.**
8. I'd **rather** get **together another** day.
9. I like **this** one better **than the other** one.
10. **Mother** must **bathe the** baby.

SELF-TEST I   (Correct answers may be found in Appendix II on p. 275.)

Read the following dialogue aloud. Circle all words that should be pronounced with the consonant [ð]. **This self-test is not on the tape.**

....

(The) Photo Album

DAUGHTER: (Mother,) I like (these) old pictures. Who's (this?)
MOTHER: That's your great grandmother.
DAUGHTER: The feathered hat is funny! Who's that man?
MOTHER: That's your grandfather. He was from the Netherlands.
DAUGHTER: I know these people! Aren't they Uncle Tom and Uncle Bob?
MOTHER: That's right. Those are my brothers. They always bothered me!
DAUGHTER: This must be either father or his brother.
MOTHER: Neither! That's your father's uncle.
DAUGHTER: Why are there other people in this photo?
MOTHER: This was a family gathering. We got together all the time.
DAUGHTER: Mother, who's this "smooth"-looking man?
MOTHER: Shhhhhhhhh! I'd rather not say. Your father will hear!
DAUGHTER: Is that your old boyfriend?
MOTHER: Well, even mothers had fun in those days!

....

After checking your answers in Appendix II, practice the dialogue again. Try it with a friend; be sure to feel your tongue between your teeth as you say the [ð] words.

FOR AN ENCORE . . . .

READING

Select a brief newspaper or magazine article. Circle all words pronounced with the consonant [ð]. Look in a mirror as you read it aloud. Be sure to see and feel the tip of your tongue between your teeth as you say [ð].

⟪IF YOU CAN SEE THE TIP OF YOUR TONGUE, YOU CAN SAY
THESE, THEM, AND *THOSE* PERFECTLY!⟫

[ʃ] as in *SHOE, NATION,* and *WISH*
(DICTIONARY MARK: sh)

PRONOUNCING [ʃ]

TIP OF TONGUE:	**near but does not touch upper gum ridge.**
MIDDLE OF TONGUE:	**near but does not touch hard palate.**
AIRSTREAM:	**is continuous without interruption.**
VOCAL CORDS:	**are not vibrating.**

POSSIBLE PRONUNCIATION PROBLEMS

The consonant [ʃ] is a familiar sound. However, you may confuse it with [tʃ] or [s].

EXAMPLE A: If you substitute [tʃ] for [ʃ]: **shoe** will sound like **chew.**
EXAMPLE B: If you substitute [s] for [ʃ]: **she** will sound like **see.**

The sound [ʃ] will be easy to produce if you round your lips and keep your airstream smooth and steady. [ʃ] **is a steady, QUIET sound. Shhhhh!**

EXERCISE A

The words on page 48 should be pronounced with [ʃ]. Repeat them after your teacher or the instructor on the tape. (Remember: Don't let your tongue touch the roof of your mouth!)

[ʃ] At the Beginning	[ʃ] In the Middle	[ʃ] At the End
shy	ocean	dish
shop	tissue	wish
ship	nation	cash
shine	patient	wash
shoe	mission	finish

[ʃ] Spelled:

"sh"	"ti"	"ci"	"ss"	"ch"
shelf	option	social	issue	chef
shirt	section	special	assure	chute
brush	fiction	musician	depression	machine

Less frequent spelling patterns for [ʃ] consist of the letters *s*, *ce*, and *xi*.

EXAMPLES: <u>s</u>ugar pen<u>s</u>ion o<u>ce</u>an an<u>xi</u>ous

---

HINTS: 1. The most common spelling pattern for [ʃ] consists of the letters *sh*.

2. The letters *t*, *ss*, and *c* before suffixes beginning with *i* are usually pronounced [ʃ].

EXAMPLES: na<u>ti</u>on profe<u>ss</u>ion so<u>ci</u>al

EXERCISE B

Repeat the following pairs of words after your teacher or the instructor on the tape. Be sure to pucker your lips for [ʃ] and form a smile for [s].

[ʃ]	[s]
ship	sip
sheet	seat
shelf	self
sheen	seen
mash	mass

EXERCISE C

The boldface words in the following phrases and sentences should be pronounced with the [ʃ] sound. Repeat them carefully after your teacher or the instructor on the tape.

1. **Shake** hands.
2. **washing machine**
3. I'm **sure**!
4. **short** on **cash**
5. **Shut** the door!
6. **Polish** your **shoes**.
7. There are many **fish** in the **ocean**.
8. The **shirt should** be **washed**.
9. We had a **short vacation** in **Washington**.
10. **She finished washing** the **dishes**.

SELF-TEST I   (Correct answers may be found in Appendix II on p. 276.)

Read each four-word series aloud. Circle the ONE word in each group of four that is **NOT** pronounced with [ʃ]. **This self-test is not on the tape.**

EXAMPLE:	(pleasure)	sure	surely	sugar
1.	crush	cash	catch	crash
2.	chef	chief	chute	chiffon
3.	machine	parachute	mustache	kitchen
4.	China	Russia	Chicago	Michigan
5.	musician	physician	chemist	electrician
6.	pressure	pressed	assure	permission
7.	division	subtraction	addition	multiplication
8.	position	action	patio	motion
9.	Charlotte	Cheryl	Sharon	Charles
10.	tension	resign	pension	mention

FOR AN ENCORE . . . .

READING

Find an advertisement for a supermarket or grocery store. Circle all items containing the [ʃ] sound.

⟪**BE SURE TO MAKE YOUR [ʃ] QUIET AND STEADY.**

SHHHHHHHHH!⟫

[ʒ] as in *MEASURE, VISION,* and *ROUGE*
(DICTIONARY MARK: zh)

PRONOUNCING [ʒ]

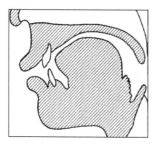

TONGUE: **is in the same position as for [ʃ].**

AIRSTREAM: **is continuous without interruption.**

VOCAL CORDS: **are vibrating.**

POSSIBLE PRONUNCIATION PROBLEMS

[ʒ] should be a familiar sound. However, it is easy to confuse with the similar English sounds [ʃ] and [dʒ].

EXAMPLE A: If you substitute [ʃ]   for [ʒ]:   **vision** will sound like **vishion**.
EXAMPLE B: If you substitute [dʒ] for [ʒ]:   **lesion** will sound like **legion**.

Be sure your vocal cords are vibrating when you say [ʒ] or you will substitute [ʃ] instead. Put your hand on your throat; FEEL THE VIBRATION! *It will be a plea_s_ure to pronounce* [ʒ].

EXERCISE A

The words on page 52 should be pronounced with [ʒ]. Repeat them accurately after your teacher or the instructor on the tape. (In English, [ʒ] does not occur at the beginning of words.)

[ʒ] In the Middle	[ʒ] At the End
Asia	rouge
vision	beige
measure	mirage
occasion	garage
decision	corsage

[ʒ] Spelled:

"si"	"su"	"gi" or "ge"
lesion	closure	regime
vision	unusual	negligee
explosion	casual	camouflage

A less frequent spelling pattern for [ʒ] consists of the letters *zu*.

EXAMPLES: a<u>zu</u>re   sei<u>zu</u>re

EXERCISE B

The boldface words in the following phrases and sentences should be pronounced with [ʒ]. Repeat them carefully after your teacher or the instructor on the tape.

1. color **television**
2. long **division**
3. That's **unusual**!
4. big **decision**
5. What's the **occasion?**
6. It's a **pleasure** to meet you.
7. The **azure** skies are **unusual.**
8. She bought a **beige negligee.**
9. We **usually** watch **television.**
10. Get a **massage** at your **leisure.**

SELF-TEST I   (Correct answers may be found in Appendix II on p. 277.)

Read each of the following sentences aloud. In the brackets provided above each boldface word, write the phonetic symbol [ʒ] or [ʃ] representing the consonant sound in that word. (Refer back to the chapter on [ʃ] as necessary.) **This self-test is not on the tape.**

EXAMPLES:
[ʃ]   [ʒ]

We will **vacation** in **Asia.**

        [   ]   [   ]

1. The **commission** made a **decision.**

            [   ]   [   ]

2. The class learned **division** and **addition.**

  [   ]   [   ]

3. **Measure** the **garage.**

      [   ]   [   ]

4. Your **profession** has **prestige.**

      [   ] [   ]   [   ]

5. That's an **unusual shade** of **rouge.**

FOR AN ENCORE ....

READING

Read *TV Guide* or the television section of the newspaper aloud one evening to your family. Underline all [ʒ] words; be sure to pronounce them carefully.

REMEMBER, KEEP PRACTICING AND . . .

⟨⟨IT WILL BE A PLEA_S_URE TO PRONOUNCE [ʒ].⟩⟩

[tʃ] as in *CHAIR, TEACHER,* and *WITCH*
(DICTIONARY MARK: ch)

PRONOUNCING [tʃ]

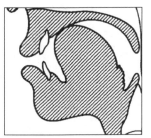

TONGUE: is firmly pressed against gum ridge behind upper front teeth.

AIRSTREAM: is stopped (as for [t]) and then released (as for [ʃ]).

VOCAL CORDS: are not vibrating.

POSSIBLE PRONUNCIATION PROBLEMS

The sounds [tʃ] and [ʃ] are easily confused with one another.

EXAMPLES: If you say [ʃ] instead of [tʃ]:   **chair** will sound like **share.**
                                                which will sound like **wish.**

Just remember to start [tʃ] with your tongue in the same place as for the sound [t]. Be sure to press your tongue tip against the gum ridge behind your upper front teeth, or you will say [ʃ] by mistake. [tʃ] is an explosive sound—like a sneeze! Think of Ah-CHOO and you'll get [tʃ] just right! **Meet the <u>ch</u>allenge of** [tʃ]!

EXERCISE A

The following words should be pronounced with [tʃ]. Repeat them after your teacher or the instructor on the tape. (Be sure to begin [tʃ] just like the sound [t].)

[tʃ] At the Beginning	[tʃ] In the Middle	[tʃ] At the End
chew	nature	itch
chair	teacher	each
chalk	picture	match
chest	hatchet	much
choose	butcher	watch

[tʃ] Spelled:

"ch"		"tu"	"tch"
chop		mature	patch
rich		culture	catch
cheap		posture	kitchen

Less frequent spelling patterns for [tʃ] consist of the letters *t* and *ti*.

EXAMPLES: righteous   digestion   question

HINT: The most common spelling pattern for [tʃ] consists of the letters *ch*.

EXERCISE B

Read the following pairs of words aloud. Be sure to press your tongue tip against the gum ridge for [tʃ] and [t] but **not** for [ʃ]. **This exercise is not on the tape.**

[tʃ]	[t]	[ʃ]
cheer	tear	sheer
chip	tip	ship
chin	tin	shin
match	mat	mash
watch	what	wash

 ## EXERCISE C

The boldface words in the following phrases and sentences should be pronounced with the consonant [tʃ]. Repeat them carefully after your teacher or the instructor on the tape. (It's important that you remember to press your tongue tip against your upper gum ridge.)

1. **Watch** out!
2. **inch** by **inch**
3. I'm **catching** a cold.
4. **cheese sandwich**
5. Don't **touch** that!
6. **chocolate chip** cookies
7. Does the **butcher charge much** for **chickens?**
8. **Which furniture** did you **choose?**
9. I **purchased** a **picture** of **China.**
10. Don't count your **chickens** before they're **hatched!**

Listen carefully as your teacher or the instructor on the tape presents five sentences. Some words that should be pronounced with [tʃ] will be said INCORRECTLY. Circle **C** for **"Correct"** or **I** for **"Incorrect"** to indicate whether the [tʃ] word in each sentence is pronounced properly.

SENTENCE	RESPONSE	
EXAMPLE A:	C Ⓘ	(Sit in the **share**.)
EXAMPLE B:	Ⓒ I	(I had to **change** a tire.)
1.	C I	
2.	C I	
3.	C I	
4.	C I	
5.	C I	

FOR AN ENCORE . . . .

CONVERSATION

Practice the phrase *"How much is it?"* Every time you have the opportunity to use this question when buying something, be sure you pronounce [tʃ] correctly.

⟨⟨MEET THE <u>CH</u>ALLENGE OF [tʃ]!⟩⟩

[dʒ] as in *JAM, MAGIC,* and *AGE*
(DICTIONARY MARK: j)

PRONOUNCING [dʒ]

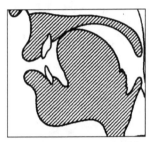

TONGUE: is in the same position as for [tʃ].

AIRSTREAM: is stopped (as for [d]) and then released (as for [ʒ]).

VOCAL CORDS: are vibrating.

POSSIBLE PRONUNCIATION PROBLEMS

Confusing English spelling patterns and similarities between [dʒ] and other sounds cause your pronunciation problems with [dʒ].

EXAMPLE A: If you substitute [j] for [dʒ]:   **jello**   will sound like **yellow.**
EXAMPLE B: If you substitute [ʒ] for [dʒ]:   **pledger** will sound like **pleasure.**
EXAMPLE C: If you substitute [tʃ] for [dʒ]:   **badge**   will sound like **batch.**

Just remember to start [dʒ] with your tongue in the same place as for the sound [d]. Be sure your tongue is pressed against your upper gum ridge **AND** that your vocal cords are vibrating when you say [dʒ]. **Just keep practicing! It will be a joy to say** [dʒ]!

EXERCISE A

The following words should be pronounced with [dʒ]. Repeat them after your teacher or the instructor on the tape. (Be sure to begin [dʒ] just like the sound [d].)

[dʒ] At the Beginning	[dʒ] In the Middle	[dʒ] At the End
jam	agent	age
joy	adjust	cage
job	magic	large
jar	enjoy	edge
gym	angel	badge

[dʒ] Spelled:

"j"	"s"	"dg"
jaw	giant	fudge
joke	gentle	budge
major	ranger	wedge

Less frequent spelling patterns for [dʒ] consist of the letters *di* and *du*.

EXAMPLES: soldier   cordial   graduate   educate

> **HINTS:**   1. The letter *j* is usually pronounced *[dʒ]*.
>
>   EXAMPLES: joke   june   January   just   John
>
>   2. The letter *g* before silent *e* at the end of a word is usually pronounced *[dʒ]*.
>
>   EXAMPLES: age   wedge   village   college

EXERCISE B

Repeat the following pairs of words after your teacher or the instructor on the tape. REMEMBER [dʒ] is a voiced sound; your vocal cords should vibrate. (Be sure to prolong any vowel BEFORE the sound [dʒ].)

[dʒ]	[tʃ]
joke	choke
gin	chin
badge	batch
ridge	rich
age	"H"

EXERCISE C

The boldface words in the following phrases and sentences should be pronounced with [dʒ]. Repeat them carefully after your teacher or the instructor on the tape.

1. **Just** a moment.
2. **Enjoy** yourself!
3. a **jar** of **jam**
4. Fourth of **July**
5. **college education**
6. **Jack** of all trades*
7. **Jim** is **just joking.**
8. **Jane enjoys jogging.**
9. **John** mailed a **large package.**
10. The **agent** took a **jet** to **Japan.**

*To be very competent or proficient in many areas.

SELF-TEST I

You're taking a jet around the world! Plan your itinerary by circling the countries pronounced with [dʒ]. **This self-test is not on the tape.**

(Java)	Guatemala	(Jerusalem)	Greece
England	Germany	Jamaica	Hungary
Japan	Greenland	Algeria	Egypt
Belgium	Argentina	China	Luxembourg

After checking your answers in Appendix II, practice the names of the countries by using them in the sentence "I'm taking a jet to _____."

FOR AN ENCORE . . . .

READING

Find a joke in a magazine or newspaper. Underline all the words containing [dʒ]. Read the joke aloud and be sure to pronounce [dʒ] correctly.

⟨⟨**JUST KEEP PRACTICING! IT WILL BE A JOY TO SAY** [dʒ]!⟩⟩

[j] as in *YOU* and *YES*
(DICTIONARY MARK: y)

PRONOUNCING [j]

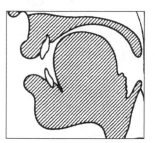

TONGUE: **is in the same position as for the vowel [i].**

AIRSTREAM: **is continuous without interruption.**

VOCAL CORDS: **are vibrating.**

POSSIBLE PRONUNCIATION PROBLEMS

The sound [j] may be a difficult sound for you to pronounce. You may confuse it with the similar sound [dʒ] or omit it.

EXAMPLE A: If you say [dʒ] instead of [j]:   **yet**   will sound like **jet.**
EXAMPLE B: If you omit [j]:   **year** will sound like **ear.**

To pronounce [j] correctly, be sure the tip of your tongue is against the back of your lower front teeth and doesn't touch the roof of your mouth. **Y̲ou'll get y̲our** [j] **sound y̲et!**

 EXERCISE A

The words on page 63 should be pronounced with [j]. Repeat them carefully after your teacher or the instructor on the tape. (In English, the consonant [j] does not occur at the end of words.)

[j] At the Beginning

yes
you
yell
use
year

[j] In the Middle

onion
canyon
lawyer
beyond
values

[j] Spelled:

"y"	"i"	"u"
yet	junior	amuse
your	senior	music
yawn	million	united

> **HINTS:** 1. The most common spelling pattern for [j] is the letter *y* followed by a vowel.
>
> EXAMPLES: <u>y</u>east <u>y</u>ou can<u>y</u>on farm<u>y</u>ard
>
> 2. When <u>y</u> is the first letter in a word, it is ALWAYS pronounced [j]; it is NEVER pronounced [dʒ].

EXERCISE B

Repeat the following pairs of words after your teacher or the instructor on the tape. REMEMBER when saying [j] to keep your tongue in the same position as for the vowel [i].

[j]	[dʒ]
Yale	jail
yolk	joke
yes	Jess
yam	jam
year	jeer

EXERCISE C

The boldface words in the following phrases and sentences should be pronounced with the consonant [j]. Repeat them carefully after your teacher or the instructor on the tape. (Be sure you **DON'T** use [dʒ] by mistake!)

1. Nice to see **you.**
2. How are **you?**
3. **Yes** or no?
4. Help **yourself.**
5. **You** look great!
6. in my **opinion**
7. Did **you** get **your** car fixed?
8. The **view** of the **canyon** is **beautiful.**
9. **You** shouldn't **yell** at **young** children.
10. Have **you** had some **yogurt yet?**

SELF-TEST I   (Correct answers may be found in Appendix II on p. 277.)

Read each of the following sentences aloud. Complete the words appropriately. **This self-test is not on the tape.**

EXAMPLES: The **young** man proposed. She said **YES**.

1. The **youth** left. He hasn't come back **YE__**.
2. The player ran 50 **yards**. The crowds began to **YE____**.
3. Today is Monday. **YE_____** was Sunday.
4. Egg **yolks** should be **YE_____**.
5. **You** should get a checkup once a **YE____**.

SELF-TEST II

(Correct answers may be found in Appendix II on p. 277.)

Listen carefully to your teacher or to the tape as five pairs of sentences are presented. Circle **SAME** if both sentences in each pair are the same. If they are NOT the same, circle **DIFFERENT**.

Pair	Response		
EXAMPLE A:	(SAME)	DIFFERENT	(He is **young**. He is **young**.)
EXAMPLE B:	SAME	(DIFFERENT)	(I heard **yes**. I heard **Jess**.)
1.	SAME	DIFFERENT	
2.	SAME	DIFFERENT	
3.	SAME	DIFFERENT	
4.	SAME	DIFFERENT	
5.	SAME	DIFFERENT	

FOR AN ENCORE . . . .

CONVERSATION

Remember to use such words as **YOU**, **YOUR**, and so on correctly in conversation. Practice such phrases as *"Nice to see YOU," "How are YOU," "Say hello to YOUR wife."*

The key to perfect pronunciation is *PRACTICE* *PRACTICE* *PRACTICE*.

⟨⟨**YOU'LL GET YOUR** [j] **SOUND YET!**⟩⟩

REVIEW EXERCISE I   [s]   [ʃ]   [t]   [tʃ]

Repeat the rows of words and sentences after your teacher or the instructor on the tape.

[s]	[ʃ]	[t]	[tʃ]
1. **S**ue	**sh**oe	**t**oo	**ch**ew
2. **s**ear	**sh**eer	**t**ear	**ch**eer
3. **s**ip	**sh**ip	**t**ip	**ch**ip
4. **s**in	**sh**in	**t**in	**ch**in
5. ma**ss**	ma**sh**	ma**t**	mat**ch**

6. Did **Sue choose** her new **shoes**?
      [s]   [tʃ]   [ʃ]

7. There's a **chip** on the **tip** of the **ship**.
         [tʃ]   [t]   [ʃ]

8. **Cass** paid **cash** for the **catch** of the day.
      [s]   [ʃ]   [tʃ]

9. **Terry** made a **cherry** pie for **Sherry**.
    [t]   [tʃ]   [ʃ]

10. **She's** eating a **cheese** **sandwich**.
     [ʃ]   [tʃ]   [s]   [tʃ]

REVIEW EXERCISE II   [s] [z] [t] [d] [θ] [ð]

Repeat the following sentences after your teacher or the instructor on the tape.

1. It's a good **faith**. It's a good **fate**. It's a good **face**. It's a good **phase**.
   [θ]   [t]   [s]   [z]

2. I went to **Beth**. I went to **bet**. I went to **Bess**. I went to **bed**.
   [θ]   [t]   [s]   [d]

3. The **raid** is set. The **rate** is set. The **race** is set. The **raise** is set.
   [d]   [t]   [s]   [z]

4. She began to **ride**. She began to **write**. She began to **writhe**.
   [d]   [t]   [ð]

   She began to **rise**.
   [z]

5. Don't **dip** it. Don't **tip** it. Don't **sip** it. Don't **zip** it.
   [d]   [t]   [s]   [z]

6. **Dan** is older **than** **Stan**.
   [d]   [ð]   [s]

7. Did you **pass** **Pat** on the **path**?
   [s]   [t]   [θ]

8. I **think** there is **zinc** in the **sink**.
   [θ]   [z]   [s]

9. **Seth** **said** to **set** the table.
   [θ]   [d]   [t]

10. **Sue** is **due** at the **zoo** at **two**.
    [s]   [d]   [z]   [t]

REVIEW EXERCISE III
Additional Contrasts

The following exercises are designed to give you practice with additional consonant sound contrasts. Repeat the following pairs of words and sentences after your teacher or the instructor on the tape.

1. **[θ]**   **[ʃ]**
   thank   **sh**ank
   thin   **sh**in
   thigh   **sh**y

2. **[ð]**   **[dʒ]**
   they   **J**ay
   than   **J**an
   though   **J**oe

3. **[z]**   **[ʒ]**
   bay**s**   bei**g**e
   ru**s**e   rou**g**e
   Cae**s**ar   sei**z**ure

4. **[z]**   **[dʒ]**
   zoo   **J**ew
   zip   **g**yp
   zone   **J**oan

5. **[ʒ]**   **[dʒ]**
   ver**s**ion   vir**g**in
   le**s**ion   le**g**ion
   plea**s**ure   ple**dg**er

6. **Jan** is younger **than** **Joe**.
   [dʒ]   [ð] [dʒ]

7. **Magicians** use **illusions** in their **shows**.
   [dʒ] [ʃ]   [ʒ]   [ʃ]

8. The **zipper** on my **jeans** is **jammed**.
   [z]   [dʒ]   [dʒ]

9. **She thinks Thelma** is **shy**.
   [ʃ]   [θ]   [θ]   [ʃ]

10. The **seizure** of **Caesar** was in **Asia**.
    [ʒ]   [z]   [ʒ]

Read the following words aloud carefully. On the lines above each word write the phonetic symbol representing the sound of the underlined letters. **This review test is not on the tape.**

Pronunciation Key: [s] as in **sit**   [d] as in **dog**
                              [z] as in **zoo** [θ] as in **think**
                              [t] as in **to**   [ð] as in **them**

                [t] [θ] [s]
EXAMPLE: too_th_pa_s_te

1. th_ou_s_and

2. s_ou_th_we_s_t

3. th_e_s_e

4. a_th_le_t_e

5. bir_th_day car_d_

After checking your answers in Appendix II, use each word in a sentence. Be sure to pronounce all consonant sounds carefully.

Your teacher or the instructor on the tape will present five three-word series. Write the number 1, 2, or 3 on the line above each word to correspond with the order of word presentation. Listen carefully to the first consonant sound in each word.

EXAMPLE: The instructor says: **sham   jam   yam**

You write: _3_   _1_   _2_

   yam   sham   jam

1. ear   jeer   year

2. cheap   jeep   sheep

3. sue   shoe   zoo

4. cello   jello   yellow

5. tease   cheese   she's

Your teacher or the instructor on the tape will present the following sentences using only ONE of the words in parentheses. Listen carefully and circle the word (and consonant) used.

EXAMPLE: The (sum   thumb) is very big.
          [s]   [θ]

1. Did you make the (bed   bet)?
                 [d]   [t]

2. We need a second (seat   sheet).
                 [s]   [ʃ]

3. Count up your (chips   tips).
               [tʃ]   [t]

4. I like to (raise   race) horses.
          [z]   [s]

5. Matthew took the (bath   bat).
               [θ]   [t]

6. (Teasing   Teething) makes the baby cry.
   [z]   [ð]

7. Before you know it, (they   Jay) will be here.
               [ð]   [dʒ]

8. Her words were spoken with (zest   jest).
               [z]   [dʒ]

After checking your answers in Appendix II, read each of the sentences twice. Carefully pronounce the first word in parentheses in the first reading and the contrast word in the second reading.

REVIEW TEST IV   (Correct answers may be found in Appendix II on p. 279.)

Pronounce the words in each of the following groups. Write the number and corresponding phonetic symbol for the sound common to each list of words at the top of the column. **This review test is not on the tape.**

Pronunciation Key:
1 = [ʃ] as in **shoe**   4 = [dʒ] as in **jam**
2 = [tʃ] as in **chair**   5 = [j] as in **you**
3 = [ʒ] as in **beige**   6 = [z] as in **zoo**

EXAMPLE: ___1___   [ʃ]
shop
shore
shout
show

1. ___ [ ]
onion
union
million
billion

2. ___ [ ]
chef
chute
chic
chiffon

3. ___ [ ]
nature
picture
capture
furniture

4. ___ [ ]
division
occasion
explosion
television

5. ___ [ ]
Russia
tissue
passion
mission

6. ___ [ ]
gradual
cordial
soldier
education

7. ___ [ ]
chief
catch
question
ketchup

8. ___ [ ]
rose
xerox
eyes
cousin
sneeze

9. ___ [ ]
cute
yawn
amuse
senior

10. ___ [ ]
ridge
angel
suggest
general

11. ___ [ ]
vision
rouge
garage
pleasure

12. ___ [ ]
season
bugs
husband
zone
maze

After checking your answers in Appendix II, practice pronouncing the preceding words again.

[p] as in *PAY, APPLE,* and *STOP*
(DICTIONARY MARK: p)

PRONOUNCING [p]

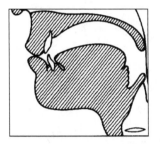

LIPS: are pressed together.

AIRSTREAM: is stopped and then exploded.

VOCAL CORDS: are not vibrating.

POSSIBLE PRONUNCIATION PROBLEMS

This is a familiar consonant to you. However, [p] is much more explosive in English than it is in other languages. When speaking English, [p] at the beginning of words must be produced with strong aspiration and a puff of air* or it might sound like [b].

EXAMPLES: If you forget to aspirate [p]:   **pear** could sound like **bear.**
                                                    pat   could sound like **bat**.

Practice saying [p] by loosely holding a tissue in front of your lips. If you aspirate [p] correctly and say it with a puff of air, your tissue will flutter. *So **PUFF, PUFF, PUFF,** and you'll pronounce a perfect [p]!*

---

*When *p* follows *s* (as in *spot, spend, spy,* etc.), it is NOT aspirated with a puff of air.

EXERCISE A

The following words should be pronounced with [p]. Repeat them after your teacher or the instructor on the tape.

[p] At the Beginning	[p] In the Middle	[p] At the End
pen	open	top
put	apart	cap
pet	apple	lip
pay	happy	map
pig	pepper	stop

EXERCISE B

The boldface words in the following phrases and sentences should be pronounced with [p]. Read them aloud carefully. *Remember to aspirate* [p] at the beginning of words! **This exercise is not on the tape.**

1. **Stop** it!
2. **pencil** and **paper**
3. a **piece** of **pie**
4. **proud** as a **peacock**
5. **Open up!**
6. **Practice** makes **perfect**.
7. The **apples** and **pears** are **ripe**.
8. The **ship** will **stop** in **Panama**.
9. Wash the **pots** and **pans** with **soap**.
10. Her **purple pants** are **pretty**.

SELF-TEST I

(Correct answers may be found in Appendix II on p. 279.)

Read the following dialogue aloud. Circle all words pronounced with [p].
This self-test is not on the tape.

∙∙∙

The (Surprise) (Trip)

PETE:	Paulette, I have a surprise! We're taking a trip tonight!
PAULETTE:	I'm very happy. But I need more time to prepare.
PETE:	That's simple. I'll help you pack.
PAULETTE:	Who will care for our pet poodle?
PETE:	Your parents!
PAULETTE:	Who will pick up the mail?
PETE:	Our neighbor Pat.
PAULETTE:	Who will water the plants?
PETE:	We'll put them on the patio.
PAULETTE:	Who will pay for the trip?
PETE:	The company is paying every penny!
PAULETTE:	Pete, you've really planned this.
PETE:	Of course! I'm dependable, superior, and a perfect. . .
PAULETTE:	"Pain in the neck!"* Don't get carried away!

∙∙∙

FOR AN ENCORE . . . .

READING

Practice the following tongue twister:

∙∙∙

Peter Piper picked a peck of pickled peppers. How many pecks of pickled peppers did Peter Piper pick? A peck!

∙∙∙

If you can master the Peter Piper tongue twister, you can say [p] perfectly!

REMEMBER TO PUFF, PUFF, PUFF, AND . . .

⟨⟨YOU'LL PRONOUNCE A PERFECT [p]!⟩⟩

*A real nuisance

[b] as in *BOY, RABBIT,* and *TUB*
(DICTIONARY MARK: b)

PRONOUNCING [b]

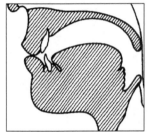

LIPS:	are pressed together (as for [p]).
AIRSTREAM:	is stopped and then exploded.
VOCAL CORDS:	are vibrating.

POSSIBLE PRONUNCIATION PROBLEMS

The consonant [b] is a simple sound for you to pronounce. However, when [b] is the last sound in a word, many speakers forget to make their vocal cords vibrate. This will make [b] sound like [p] and confuse your listeners.

EXAMPLES: If you say [p] instead of [b]:   **robe** will sound like **rope**.
cab   will sound like **cap**.

The consonant [b] will be easy to say if you make your vocal cords vibrate and firmly press your lips together. ***BE sure to say* [b] *with a BOOM and you'll BE at your BEST!***

EXERCISE A

The following words should be pronounced with [b]. Repeat them after your teacher or the instructor on the tape.

[b] At the Beginning	[b] In the Middle	[b] At the End
be	obey	cab
but	baby	cub
bat	habit	tub
back	cabin	knob
best	neighbor	bulb

> **HINTS:** 1. The letter *b* is almost always pronounced [b]. (Note the exception described in the following hint.)
>
> 2. When *b* follows *m* in the same syllable, it is usually NOT pronounced.
>
> EXAMPLES: comb bomb lamb plumber

EXERCISE B

Repeat the following pairs of words after your teacher or the instructor on the tape. (Make certain that your lips are pressed together and that you add "voicing" when saying [b].)

[b]	[p]
mob	mop
tab	tap
cab	cap
pub	pup
symbol	simple

EXERCISE C

Read the following phrases and sentences aloud. Remember, the boldface words should be pronounced with the voiced consonant [b]. **This exercise is not on the tape.**

1. **bread** and **butter**
2. **above** and **below**
3. **baseball** game
4. **black** and **blue**
5. the **bigger** the **better**
6. I'll **be back**.
7. **Bad habits** can **be broken**.
8. **Bill** is in the **lobby**.
9. **Bob bought** a **blue bathrobe**.
10. **Betty** was **born** in **Boston**.

SELF-TEST I   (Correct answers may be found in Appendix II on p.280.)

Read the following dialogue aloud. Circle all words pronounced with [b]. **This self-test is not on the tape.**

....

BETTY: (Ben,) I bet you forgot my birthday!
BEN: I bet I didn't. I bought you a birthday present.
BETTY: I can't believe it. What did you bring?
BEN: It begins with the letter **B**.
BETTY: Oh, boy! It must be a bathrobe. You buy me one every birthday.
BEN: It's not a bathrobe!
BETTY: Is it a bowling ball?
BEN: No, it's not a bowling ball.
BETTY: It must be a book about boating, your favorite hobby.
BEN: Betty, you're way off base. I bought you a bracelet. A diamond bracelet!
BETTY: Wow! This is the best birthday present I ever got. You didn't rob a bank, did you?
BEN: Don't worry. I didn't beg, borrow, or steal; just don't expect any more presents for a long time. I'm broke!

....

FOR AN ENCORE . . . .

CONVERSATION

On your next three visits to a **boutique** or department store, be sure to tell the salesperson, "I'd like to **buy** a _____" (**black blouse, blue belt**, etc.). After each purchase, tell a friend or family member, "I **bought** a _____." Be sure to pronounce [b] correctly.

SAY [b] **WITH A BOOM AND . . .**

⟨⟨**YOU'LL BE AT YOUR BEST!**⟩⟩

[f] as in *FUN, OFFICE,* and *IF*
(DICTIONARY MARK: f)

PRONOUNCING [f]

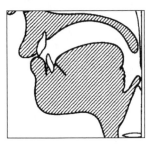

UPPER TEETH:	touch lower lip.
AIRSTREAM:	is continuous without interruption.
VOCAL CORDS:	are not vibrating.

POSSIBLE PRONUNCIATION PROBLEMS

The sound [f] should be produced with the upper teeth touching the lower lip. Some international students tend to keep their lips apart and produce a sound similar to [h]. Others completely close their lips and make the sound [p].

EXAMPLE A: If you say [h] instead of [f]: **fat** will sound like **hat**.
EXAMPLE B: If you say [p] instead of [f]: **cuff** will sound like **cup**.

Just be sure your upper teeth are touching your lower lip and ***your* [f] *will be PERFECTLY FINE!***

EXERCISE A

The following words should be pronounced with [f]. Repeat them after your teacher or the instructor on the tape.

[f] At the Beginning	[f] In the Middle	[f] At the End
for	safe	if
few	offer	off
fast	after	half
five	office	safe
face	coffee	cough

[f] Spelled:

"f"	"ph"	"gh"
fat	phone	rough
fine	phrase	tough
foot	Philip	laugh
first	nephew	cough
stiff	physical	enough

> **HINTS:**   1. The letter *f* is usually pronounced [f].
>
>   2. The letters *ph* are usually pronounced [f].
>
>   EXAMPLES: photo   telephone   graph

EXERCISE B

Read the following pairs of words aloud. Your upper teeth should contact your lower lip for [f] and your vocal cords should **NOT** vibrate. **This exercise is not on the tape.**

[f]	[p]
fine	pine
face	pace
calf	cap
leaf	leap
puff	pup

EXERCISE C

The boldface words in the following phrases and sentences should be pronounced with [f]. Read them aloud as accurately as possible. **This exercise is not on the tape.**

1. **half** past **four**
2. **before** or **after**
3. **face** the **facts**
4. I'm **feeling fine**.
5. Do me a **favor**.
6. Answer the **phone**.
7. Are you **free** on **Friday afternoon**?
8. The **office** is on the **first floor**.
9. That **fellow** has a **familiar face**.
10. Do you **prefer fish** or **fowl**?

SELF-TEST I
(Correct answers may be found in Appendix II on p. 280.)

Read the following directions and answer them aloud with the appropriate [f] word from the list. **This self-test is not on the tape.**

graph   photograph   phone   phonetics   philosopher
pharmacy   nephew   phonograph physician   prophet

1. **Find** another name **for** a drugstore. _____
2. **Find** another name **for** a doctor. _____
3. **Find** another name **for** a snapshot. _____
4. **Find** the name **for** a person who studies **philosophy**. _____
5. **Find** the short **form** of the word *telephone*. _____
6. **Find** another name **for** a record player. _____
7. **Find** the name **for** a person who predicts the **future**. _____
8. **Find** the name **for** the study of sounds. _____
9. **Find** the term that **refers** to your sister's son. _____
10. **Find** the name for a chart showing **figures**. _____

SELF-TEST II
(Correct answers may be found in Appendix II on p. 280.)

Read the following paragraph aloud. Circle all words that should be pronounced with the consonant [f]. (Be sure your upper teeth touch your lower lip as you say [f].) **This self-test is not on the tape.**

Florida was founded by Ponce de Leon in 1513. This famous explorer from Spain was searching for a fountain of youth. He named the land *Florida*, which means "full of flowers" in Spanish. He failed in his efforts to find the fountain. He finally died after fighting the Indians. Unfortunately, no one has ever found the fountain in Florida or the formula for eternal youth. However, the fun and sun in Florida are enough to attract folks from every hemisphere to this famous American state.

After checking your answers in Appendix II, read the paragraph aloud one more time.

FOR AN ENCORE . . . .

READING

Find your horoscope in the local newspaper. Circle all words pronounced with [f]. Read your *"fortune"* aloud to a friend!

KEEP PRACTICING AND . . .

⟨⟨YOUR [f] WILL BE PERFECTLY FINE!⟩⟩

[v] as in *VERY, OVER,* and *SAVE*
(DICTIONARY MARK: v)

PRONOUNCING [v]

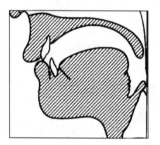

UPPER TEETH: touch the lower lip (as for [f]).

AIRSTREAM: is continuous without interruption.

VOCAL CORDS: are vibrating.

POSSIBLE PRONUNCIATION PROBLEMS

1. International students frequently substitute [b] for [v] when speaking English. This will greatly confuse the listener!

    EXAMPLES: If you say [b] instead of [v]: **very** will sound like **berry**.
    vest will sound like **best**.

2. When [v] is the last sound in a word, many speakers forget to vibrate their vocal cords. This will make [v] sound like [f] and confuse your listeners.

    EXAMPLES: If you say [f] instead of [v]: **save** will sound like **safe**.
    leave will sound like **leaf**.

The sound [v] will be easy for you to say if you CONCENTRATE on placing your upper teeth over your bottom lip. ***LOOK IN THE MIRROR* as you practice the [v] exercises** and remember to make your vocal cords vibrate. ***Your* [v] *will be <u>VERY</u> good!***

EXERCISE A

The following words should be pronounced with [v]. Repeat them after your teacher or the instructor on the tape. (Be sure you feel your upper teeth touch your lower lip.)

[v] At the Beginning	[v] In the Middle	[v] At the End
vine	even	of
vase	over	have
vote	seven	move
vest	heavy	stove
very	movie	carve

> **HINT:** The letter *v* in English is always pronounced [v]. A less common spelling for [v] is the letter *f*.
>
> EXAMPLE: o*f*

EXERCISE B

Repeat the following pairs of words after your teacher or the instructor on the tape. Place your upper teeth over your bottom lip and add voicing for [v]. (Be sure to prolong any vowel BEFORE the sound [v].)

I		II	
[v]	**[b]**	**[v]**	**[f]**
vest	best	save	safe
vow	bow	leave	leaf
very	berry	have	half
marvel	marble	believe	belief
vase	base	live	life

EXERCISE C

The boldface words in the following phrases and sentences should be pronounced with the consonant [v]. Repeat them carefully after your teacher or the instructor on the tape.

1. **very** good
2. **very** nice
3. **Very** truly yours
4. **Move over**!
5. **over** and **over**
6. **seventh of November**
7. **Have** you **ever** been to **Venice**?
8. The **vase** is **very** heavy.
9. **Eve** has a **severe fever**.
10. **Move** the **TV over** here.

SELF-TEST I   (Correct answers may be found in Appendix II on p. 281.)

Listen carefully to your teacher or to the tape as five words pronounced with [v] are presented. Indicate whether you hear the [v] sound at the **Beginning (B), Middle (M),** or **End (E)** of the word.

EXAMPLE: The instructor says: **saving**
You circle: B Ⓜ E

1. B M E
2. B M E
3. B M E
4. B M E
5. B M E

SELF-TEST II   (Correct answers may be found in Appendix II on p. 281.)

Read aloud the following poem by Emily Dickinson. Circle all words that should be pronounced with the consonant [v]. **This self-test is not on the tape.**

··

I (Never) Saw a Moor

I never saw a moor,
I never saw the sea;
Yet know I how the heather looks,
And what a wave must be.

I never spoke with God,
Nor visited in Heaven;
Yet certain am I of the spot
As if the chart were given.

(Emily Dickinson)

··

FOR AN ENCORE ·

CONVERSATION

Everyone likes to be complimented or praised! Plan on complimenting at least five people this week by using such phrases as "**very** good," "**very** nice," "You look **very** well," "You **have** a **very** pretty **vest**," and so on.

KEEP PRACTICING EVERY DAY AND . . .

⟨⟨YOUR [v] WILL BE <u>V</u>ERY GOOD!⟩⟩

[h] as in *HAT* and *BEHIND*
(DICTIONARY MARK: h)

PRONOUNCING [h]

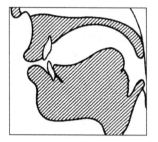

TONGUE: glides into position for whichever vowel follows [h].

AIRSTREAM: is continuous.

VOCAL CORDS: are not vibrating.

POSSIBLE PRONUNCIATION PROBLEMS

The sound [h] is a familiar sound. However, some speakers substitute [f] and [ʃ] for [h] before the vowels [u] and [i].

EXAMPLE A: If you substitute [ʃ] for [h]: **heat** will sound like **sheet**.
EXAMPLE B: If you substitute [f] for [h]: **Hugh** will sound like **few**.

This is a very easy sound to produce. Relax your throat and tongue; GENTLY let out a puff of air as if you were sighing. ***Work _hard_ and you'll be _happy_ with [h]!***

EXERCISE A

The following words should be pronounced with [h]. Repeat them after your teacher or the instructor on the tape. *(Remember—let out a GENTLE puff of air as you say [h].)*

[h] At the Beginning   **[h] In the Middle**

[h] At the Beginning	[h] In the Middle
he	ahead
how	behind
who	behave
here	inhale
heat	anyhow

A less frequent spelling pattern for [h] is *wh*.

EXAMPLES: who   whom   whose   whole

> **HINTS:**   1. The letter *h* is silent when it follows *g, k,* or *r* at the beginning of words.
>
>   EXAMPLES: ghost   khaki   rhubarb
>
>   2. The letter *h* is always silent in the words *honest, heir, honor,* and *hour.*

EXERCISE B

Repeat the following three-word groups after your teacher or the instructor on the tape. Be sure your lips are completely apart for the [h] words.

[h]	[f]	[s]
he	fee	she
heat	feet	sheet
hear	fear	sheer
head	fed	shed
Hugh	few	shoe

EXERCISE C

Read the following phrases and sentences aloud. The boldface words should be pronounced with [h]. **This exercise is not on the tape.**

1. **Hurry** up!
2. What **happened**?
3. **Who** is it?
4. **hand** in **hand**
5. **How have** you been?
6. You **hit** the nail on the **head**!*
7. **Henry hit** a **home** run.
8. **He had hot** dogs and **hamburgers**.
9. **Who** lives **behind** the **house**?
10. **Helen has** brown **hair**.

SELF-TEST I (Correct answers may be found in Appendix II on p. 281.)

Guess what? You're *HAVING* a *HOLIDAY*! Plan your tour by circling the places pronounced with [h]. **This self-test is not on the tape.**

(Ohio)	Michigan	Oklahoma	Houston
Idaho	Massachusetts	Washington	New Hampshire
Chicago	Hartford	Hawaii	Tallahassee

After checking your answers in Appendix II, practice the names of these places by using them in the sentence "I'm **having** a **holiday** in _____."

*To be perfectly accurate.

SELF-TEST II   (Correct answers may be found in Appendix II on p. 281.)

Read the following dialogue aloud. Circle all words pronounced with [h]. **This self-test is not on the tape.**

....

HELEN: (Hi) Mom. Welcome (home.) How was Hawaii?
MOTHER: Like a second honeymoon! I'm as happy as a lark. How are
          you?
HELEN: Horrible! Henry is in the hospital with a broken hip.
MOTHER: How did that happen?
HELEN: He heard a noise outside. He went behind the house and fell
          over a hose.
MOTHER: How are my handsome grandsons?
HELEN: They won't behave. And my housekeeper had to quit.
MOTHER: Perhaps you'd like me to help at home.
HELEN: Oh, Mom, I was hoping you'd say that. Hurry to the house as
          soon as possible.
MOTHER: I guess the honeymoon is over. Here we go again!

....

After checking your answers in Appendix II, read the dialogue again. Be sure to aspirate all [h] words with a gentle puff of air.

⟨⟨WORK **H**ARD AND YOU'LL BE **H**APPY WITH [h]!⟩⟩

[w] as in *WE* and *AWAY*
(DICTIONARY MARK: w)

PRONOUNCING [w]

LIPS: are rounded and in the same position as for the vowel [u].

AIRSTREAM: is continuous.

VOCAL CORDS: are vibrating.

POSSIBLE PRONUNCIATION PROBLEMS

1. It is easy to confuse [w] with [v]. If you make this error it can completely change the meaning of the word you are saying.

   EXAMPLES: If you substitute [v] for [w]: **went** will sound like **vent**.
   wheel will sound like **veal**.

2. Speakers of other languages sometimes omit [w] before the vowels [u] or [ʊ].

   EXAMPLES: If you omit [w]: **wool** will sound like **ool**.
   wood will sound like **ood**.

As you start to produce the consonant [w], remember to completely round your lips as for [u]. Be sure your lower lip does NOT touch your upper teeth or you'll make a [v] instead. ***Don't worry! Keep working away and your* [w] *will be wonderful!***

The following words should be pronounced with [w]. Repeat them after your teacher or the instructor on the tape. *Be sure to round your **lips fully.*** (The consonant sound [w] does not occur at the end of words in English.)

[w] In the Beginning	[w] In the Middle
we	away
was	awake
want	anyway
woman	between
would	someone

Less frequent spelling patterns for [w] consist of the letters *o* and *u*.

EXAMPLES: <u>o</u>ne any<u>o</u>ne q<u>u</u>een q<u>u</u>iet

> **HINTS:** 1. The letter *w* is always pronounced [w] when followed by a vowel in the same syllable.
>
> EXAMPLES: <u>w</u>ood <u>w</u>ill back<u>w</u>ard high<u>w</u>ay
>
> 2. The letter *w* at the end of a word is always *silent*.
>
> EXAMPLES: how sew law know

EXERCISE B

Read the following pairs of words aloud. Be sure to completely **round** your lips for the [w] words. **This exercise is not on the tape.**

[w]	[v]
wine	vine
went	vent
west	vest
while	vile
wow	vow

EXERCISE C

The boldface words in the following phrases and sentences should be pronounced with [w]. Read them aloud as accurately as possible. **This exercise is not on the tape.**

1. **What** do you **want**?
2. You're **welcome**.
3. **Where will** you be?
4. **Walk quickly**.
5. **Where** is it?
6. **Waste** not, **want** not!
7. **Which one** do you **want**?
8. **What was** the **question**?
9. The **women were wearing white**.
10. **Walt always works** on **Wednesday**.

SELF-TEST I   (Correct answers may be found in Appendix II on p. 282.)

Read the following paragraph about Woodrow Wilson aloud. Circle all words that should be pronounced with [w]. **This self-test is not on the tape.**

●●

(Woodrow) (Wilson)

   Woodrow Wilson was the twenty-fifth president of the United States. He will always be remembered for his work to establish world peace. Wilson was born in 1865 and later went to Princeton University. He became president in 1913 and stayed in the White House for two terms. His first wife died while he was in office, and he married a Washington widow. When the United States entered World War I in 1917, Wilson quickly provided the needed wisdom. After the war, Wilson made a nationwide tour to win support for the League of Nations. Wilson was awarded the Nobel Prize for his worthwhile work for peace. He died in 1924. Everywhere in the world, Wilson was thought of as a wise and wonderful leader.

●●

SELF-TEST II (Correct answers may be found in Appendix II on p. 282.)

Read the following questions about Woodrow Wilson aloud. Fill in the blanks with the correct answers. Be sure to pronounce all [w] words correctly. **This self-test is not on the tape**.

1. **When <u>w</u>as <u>W</u>oodrow <u>W</u>ilson** born?
   <u>W</u>oodrow <u>W</u>ilson <u>w</u>as born in _____.

2. How many **<u>w</u>ives** did **<u>W</u>ilson** have **<u>w</u>hile** in the **<u>W</u>hite** House?
   <u>W</u>ilson had _____ **<u>w</u>ives**.

3. **<u>W</u>hen** did the United States enter **<u>W</u>orld <u>W</u>ar I?**
   The United States entered **<u>W</u>orld <u>W</u>ar I** in _____.

4. **<u>W</u>hy <u>w</u>as <u>W</u>ilson a<u>w</u>arded** the Nobel Prize?
   <u>W</u>ilson <u>w</u>as a<u>w</u>arded the Nobel Prize for his _____.

5. **<u>W</u>here <u>w</u>as <u>W</u>ilson** thought of as a **<u>w</u>ise** and **<u>w</u>onderful** leader?
   <u>W</u>ilson <u>w</u>as thought of as a **<u>w</u>ise** and **<u>w</u>onderful** leader _____.

FOR AN ENCORE . . . .

CONVERSATION

Most questions begin with the [w] sound. AL<u>W</u>AYS pronounce [w] correctly when you ask *Where? When? Why? Which one? Will you? Won't you?* and so on.

KEEP <u>W</u>ORKING AND

⟨⟨YOUR [w] <u>W</u>ILL BE <u>W</u>ONDERFUL!⟩⟩

96   [w] as in we

REVIEW EXERCISE

Repeat the rows of words and sentences after your teacher or the instructor on the tape.

[b]	[v]	[w]
1. **b**ail	**v**eil	**wh**ale
2. **b**et	**v**et	**w**et
3. **b**ow	**v**ow	**w**ow
4. **b**est	**v**est	**w**est
5. **b**uy	**v**ie	**wh**y

[f]	[h]	[p]
6. **f**it	**h**it	**p**it
7. **f**at	**h**at	**p**at
8. **f**eet	**h**eat	**P**ete
9. **f**air	**h**air	**p**ear
10. **ph**ase	**h**aze	**p**ays

11. The **heat hurt Pete's feet**
    [h] [h] [p]   [f]

12. **We'll** eat **veal** and **beans**.
    [w]   [v]   [b]

13. Get the **pan** and **fan from** the **van**.
        [p]   [f] [f]   [v]

14. **Hugh had few fights.**
    [h]   [h] [f] [f]

15. Did you **leave** your **cap** in the **cab**?
        [v]   [p]   [b]

Your teacher or the instructor on the tape will present the following sentences using ONE of the words in parentheses. Listen carefully and circle the word (and consonant) used.

EXAMPLE: We bought a new (fan   van).
                          [f]   [v]

1. Vera took a   (bow   vow).
                        [b]   [v]

2. That's a nice   (beach   peach).
                        [b]   [p]

3. There were a lot of (boats   votes).
                        [b]   [v]

4. We could see her   (grief   grieve).
                        [f]   [v]

5. I want the   (vest   best).
                        [v]   [b]

After checking your answers in Appendix II, read each of the sentences twice. Use the first word in the first reading and the contrast word in the second reading.

(Correct answers may be found in Appendix II on p. 282.)

Listen carefully to your teacher or to the tape as five sentences are presented. One word in each sentence will be INCORRECTLY pronounced. On the line to the right of each number, write the CORRECT word for each sentence.

	Correct Word	Sentence
EXAMPLE A:	feet	(She wore sneakers on her **heat**.)
EXAMPLE B:	west	(We took a trip to the **vest** coast.)

1. _____
2. _____
3. _____
4. _____
5. _____

REVIEW TEST III   (Correct answers may be found in Appendix II on p. 283.)

Read the following definition and FABLE aloud. Underline all the words pronounced with [p], [b], [f], [v], [h], and [w]. Write them under the correct phonetic symbols on page 100. **This review test is not on the tape.**

Definition of _fable_: A <u>fable</u> is a story that teaches a valuable lesson. Aesop's fables are very <u>well</u> known. <u>His</u> brief stories tell <u>of</u> the faults and virtues of people.

•••

The Fox and the Grapes

Once there was a very hungry fox. He saw some fine grapes hanging above from a vine. He tried jumping up, but he couldn't reach the grapes. Finally, he became furious and gave up. As he left, the fox said, "I didn't really want those grapes. They were probably sour!"

(by Aesop)

•••

The next time somebody pretends he doesn't want something because he really can't have it, you can say "sour grapes!"

[p]	[b]	[f]
	fa<u>b</u>le	de<u>f</u>inition <u>f</u>able
[v]	[h]	[w]
o<u>f</u>	<u>h</u>is	<u>w</u>ell

[k] as in *CAKE, CAR,* and *BOOK*
(DICTIONARY MARK: k)

PRONOUNCING [k]

BACK OF TONGUE: touches the soft palate.

AIRSTREAM: is stopped and then exploded.

VOCAL CORDS: are not vibrating.

POSSIBLE PRONUNCIATION PROBLEMS

This is an easy consonant for you to say. Just remember that [k] is very explosive in English. When it begins a word, it must be said with strong aspiration and a puff of air.* ***Keep pra̱cticing. You c̱an say [k] OK!***

 # EXERCISE A

The following words should be pronounced with [k]. Repeat them after your teacher or the instructor on the tape.

[k] At the Beginning	[k] In the Middle	[k] At the End
can	cookie	took
key	become	week
keep	jacket	sick
come	walking	make
quick	because	speak

*When *k* follows *s* (as in *sky, skin, skate,* etc.), it is NOT aspirated with a puff of air.

[k] Spelled:

"k"	"c"	"qu" ([kw])	"x" ([ks])
kite	coat	quit	six
kill	cone	quick	box
lake	acre	quiet	wax
keep	class	quote	exit
bake	crime	square	mixture

A less frequent spelling pattern for [k] consists of the letters *ch*.

EXAMPLES: <u>ch</u>orus   <u>ch</u>rome   me<u>ch</u>anic   <u>Ch</u>ristmas

---

HINTS: 1. The most common spelling pattern for [k] is *k*.

2. The letters *qu* are usually pronounced [kw].

   EXAMPLES: <u>qu</u>een   <u>qu</u>ite   re<u>qu</u>ire

3. The letter *c* before *a*, *o*, or *u* is usually pronounced [k].

   EXAMPLES: <u>c</u>ap   be<u>c</u>ause   <u>c</u>omb   be<u>c</u>ome   <u>c</u>ut

4. The letter *k* followed by *n* is usually NOT pronounced.

   EXAMPLES: knit [nɪt]   knot [nɑt]   know [noʊ]

Read the following paragraph aloud. Circle all words that should be pronounced with [k]. **This self-test is not on the tape.**

· ·

The (American)(Cowboy)

    Americans created the name *cowboy* for the men who cared for the cattle. You might recall the typical singing cowboy in the movies. He was kind, courageous, and good looking. He always caught the cow, colt, and of course, the girl! But the real cowboy was a hard worker who had many difficult tasks. He had to take the cattle to market. These lonely cattle drives took many weeks through rough country. The cowboy had to protect the cattle and keep them from running off. In fact or fiction, the cowboy will continue to be a likeable American character. ***Ride 'em cowboy!***

· ·

After checking your answers in Appendix II, practice reading **"The American Cowboy"** again.

FOR AN ENCORE ·

CONVERSATION

Ask new people you meet, *"What **kind** of **work** do you do?"* Every time you ask for a "***cup** of **black coffee***" or "***coffee** with **milk** or **cream**,*" ***carefully*** pronounce **[k]**!

KEEP PRA<u>C</u>TICING AND . . .

⟨⟨YOU <u>C</u>AN SAY [k] O<u>K</u>!⟩⟩

[g] as in *GO, BEGIN,* and *EGG*
(DICTIONARY MARK: g)

PRONOUNCING [g]

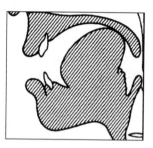

BACK OF TONGUE: touches the soft palate.

AIRSTREAM: is stopped and then exploded.

VOCAL CORDS: are vibrating.

POSSIBLE PRONUNCIATION PROBLEMS

This should be a familiar sound. However, when [g] is the last sound in a word, you might forget to add voicing or substitute [ŋ]. This will change the meaning of your words.

EXAMPLE A: If you substitute [k] for [g]:   **bag** will sound like **back**.
EXAMPLE B: If you substitute [ŋ] for [g]:   **rug** will sound like **rung**.

Always make your vocal cords vibrate for [g] at the end of words. Let your [g] <u>G</u>O with an explosion. **Your [g] has <u>G</u>OT to be <u>G</u>OOD!**

EXERCISE A

The following words should be pronounced with [g]. Repeat them after your teacher or the instructor on the tape. Be sure to make your vocal cords vibrate.

[g] At the Beginning	[g] In the Middle	[g] At the End
go	cigar	beg
get	begin	pig
gone	anger	bag
guess	forget	dog
gather	bigger	egg

[g] Spelled:

"g"	"x" ([gz])
go	exact
give	exam
game	example
forgive	exert
regain	exhibit

EXERCISE B

Read aloud the following pairs of words. (Be sure to make your vocal cords vibrate for [g] and to prolong any vowel BEFORE the sound [g].) **This exercise is not on the tape.**

[g]	[k]
bag	back
pig	pick
log	lock
dug	duck
tag	tack

EXERCISE C

The boldface words in the following phrases and sentences should be pronounced with [g]. Read them aloud as accurately as possible. **This exercise is not on the tape.**

1. **good** night
2. I don't **agree**.
3. Where are you **going**?
4. **begin again**
5. a **good girl**
6. a **big dog**
7. **Peggy** is **going** to the **game**.
8. The **dog dug** up his bone **again**.
9. Don't kill the **goose** that lays the **golden egg**.
10. There's a **big bug** on the **rug**.

 **SELF-TEST I**   (Correct answers may be found in Appendix II on p. 283.)

Your teacher or the instructor on the tape will say only ONE word in each of the following pairs. Listen carefully and circle the word you hear.

EXAMPLE A: (wig)   wick

EXAMPLE B: tug   (tuck)

1. lag   lack
2. bug   buck
3. league   leak
4. peg   peck
5. nag   knack

SELF-TEST II
(Correct answers may be found in Appendix II on p. 284.)

Mr. and Mrs. **Green** are planning a menu for their **guests**. They will serve only foods pronounced with [g]. Read the menu and circle all items pronounced with [g]. **This self-test is not on the tape.**

BREAKFAST

Grapefruit	Eggs	Yogurt	Sausage

LUNCH

Hamburgers	Grilled Onions	Gelatin	Vinegar Dressing

COCKTAILS

Margarita	Gin and Tonic	Burgundy Wine	Grand Marnier

DINNER

Lasagna	Leg of Lamb	Green Peas	Gumbo

DESSERT

Angel Food Cake	Sugar Cookies	Grapes	Figs

After checking your answers in Appendix II, practice each circled [g] menu item by saying it in the sentence **"I'm GOING to eat _____."**
Be sure to pronounce all [g] menu items correctly!

FOR AN ENCORE ·

CONVERSATION

Every time you use the word **GOOD** in conversation ("**Good** morning," "You look **good**," "Did you have a **good** time?" etc.) be sure to pronounce [g] correctly.

⟨⟨YOUR [g] has GOT TO BE GOOD!⟩⟩

[m] as in *ME* and *SWIM*
(DICTIONARY MARK: m)

PRONOUNCING [m]

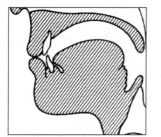

LIPS:	are together in a "humming" position.
AIRSTREAM:	is continuous through the nose.
VOCAL CORDS:	are vibrating.

POSSIBLE PRONUNCIATION PROBLEMS

This is a familiar sound to you; it will be easy to say in the beginning and middle of words. However, you might substitute the more familiar [n] or [ŋ] at the end of the words in English.

EXAMPLE A: If you say [n] instead of [m]:   **some** will become **sun**.
EXAMPLE B: If you say [ŋ] instead of [m]:   **swim** will become **swing**.

Remember, make your lips come together in a "humming" position for [m]. Say "mmmmmmmmm" and your [m] will be marvelous!

EXERCISE A

The following words should be pronounced with [m]. Repeat them after your teacher or the instructor on the tape. *(Remember—lips together!)*

[m] At the Beginning	[m] In the Middle	[m] At the End
me	among	am
may	summer	him
mat	hammer	them
mean	mailman	seem
month	something	name

EXERCISE B

The boldface words in the following phrases and sentences should be pronounced with [m]. Read them aloud as accurately as possible. ***Remember, KEEP YOUR LIPS TOGETHER*** *(especially when [m] is the last sound in the word).* **This exercise is not on the tape.**

1. **arm** in **arm**
2. **lemon** and **lime**
3. **summertime**
4. What's your **name**?
5. What **time** is it?
6. Don't **blame me**!
7. What **time** is **my appointment**?
8. Tell **them** to **come home**.
9. **Tim** is **from** a **farm**.
10. Give **Pam some more ham**.

SELF-TEST I

(Correct answers may be found in Appendix II on p. 284.)

Listen carefully to your teacher or instructor on the tape as five pairs of words are presented. ONE word in each pair is pronounced with [m]. Circle the number of the word with [m].

EXAMPLE: The instructor says: ***some   sun***

You circle: ①   2

1. 1 2
2. 1 2
3. 1 2
4. 1 2
5. 1 2

FOR AN ENCORE . . . .

CONVERSATION

Every time you meet someone new, be sure to use the phrase "***What's your na**m**e?***" correctly. If someone asks your name be sure to respond, "***My na**m**e is . . .***"

《REMEMBER TO SAY "m̲mmmmmmmmmmmmmmm"

AND YOUR [m] WILL BE MARVELOUS!》

110 [m] as in me

[n] as in *NO* and *RUN*
(DICTIONARY MARK: n)

PRONOUNCING [n]

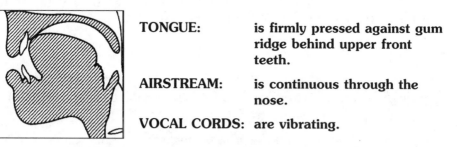

TONGUE:	**is firmly pressed against gum ridge behind upper front teeth.**
AIRSTREAM:	**is continuous through the nose.**
VOCAL CORDS:	**are vibrating.**

POSSIBLE PRONUNCIATION PROBLEMS

Because of the similarity of the nasal consonants [m], [n], and [ŋ], speakers of other languages frequently confuse them in English, particularly at the end of words.

EXAMPLE A: If you say [m] instead of [n]: **sun** will sound like **some**.
EXAMPLE B: If you say [ŋ] instead of [n]: **ran** will sound like **rang**.

ALWAYS press your tongue tip firmly against the gum ridge behind your upper front teeth, *especially at the end of words.* ***Practice this SOUND AGAIN and AGAIN; you'll have a FINE PRONUNCIATION of* [n]*!***

EXERCISE A

The words on page 112 should be pronounced with [n]. Repeat them after your teacher or the instructor on the tape. *(Remember—tongue tip up!)*

[n] At the Beginning	[n] In the Middle	[n] At the End
no	any	in
new	many	on
net	money	can
know	window	when
knee	banana	then

NOTE ABOUT "SYLLABIC [n]": When an unstressed syllable begins with [t] or [d] and ends with [n], the [n] is frequently pronounced as "syllabic [n]." It is formed by keeping the tongue tip on the upper gum ridge without moving it from the position of the preceding [t] or [d].

EXAMPLES: sadden kitten curtain beaten rotten sudden

HINTS: 1. The letter *n* is almost always pronounced [n]. (Note the exception described in the following hint.)

2. When *n* follows *m* in the same syllable, it is usually NOT pronounced.

EXAMPLES: column solemn hymn autumn

EXERCISE B

The boldface words in the following phrases and sentences should be pronounced with [n]. Read them aloud carefully. ***Remember, tongue tip up*** (especially when [n] is the last sound in a word). **This exercise is not on the tape.**

1. **Answer** the **phone**.
2. Come **again**.
3. **rain** or **shine**
4. I **don't know**.
5. **Open** the **window**.
6. Leave me **alone**.
7. **Dinner** is between **seven** and **nine**.
8. **Dan** is a **fine man**.
9. **Ben** will be **on** the **ten** o'clock **train**.
10. Come **down when** you **can**.

Listen carefully to your teacher or the tape as five pairs of sentences are presented. Circle **S** if both sentences in the pair are the **SAME**. If they are **DIFFERENT**, circle **D**.

Sentence Pair	Response
EXAMPLE A:	S (D) (Is it **Tim**? It is **tin**?)
EXAMPLE B:	(S) D (I feel **fine.** I feel **fine.**)
1.	S D
2.	S D
3.	S D
4.	S D
5.	S D

FOR AN ENCORE . . . .

READING

Select a paragraph from a book you are reading. Circle the words **IN, ON, THEN, THAN,** and **CAN** each time they are used. Practice reading aloud; be sure to pronounce them correctly.

《《**PRACTICE THIS SOUND AGAIN AND AGAIN!**》》

[ŋ] as in *SING*
(DICTIONARY MARK: ŋ)

PRONOUNCING [ŋ]

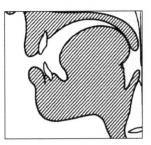

BACK OF TONGUE: is raised toward the soft palate.

AIRSTREAM: is continuous through the nose.

VOCAL CORDS: are vibrating.

POSSIBLE PRONUNCIATION PROBLEMS

Many international students are unaccustomed to pronouncing [ŋ] at the end of words. Also, the similarity between [ŋ] and [n] might confuse you.

EXAMPLES: If you say [n] instead of [ŋ]:   **feeling** will sound like "**feelin**."
                                                                    sing   will sound like **sin**.

The key to pronouncing [ŋ] correctly is to raise the BACK of your tongue— NOT the TIP! *Just keep study<u>ing</u>, think<u>ing</u>, and practic<u>ing</u>; everyth<u>ing</u> will be OK with* [ŋ]*!*

EXERCISE A

The following words should be pronounced with [ŋ]. Repeat them carefully after your teacher or the instructor on the tape.

[ŋ] In the Middle

anger
thank
finger
banging
youngest

[ŋ] At the End

sting
tongue
walking
feeling
singing

> *HINTS:*   1. The letters *ng* or *ngue* at the end of words are ALWAYS pronounced [ŋ].
>
>   EXAMPLES: wrong   sing   walking   tongue
>
>   2. The letter *n* before *g* or *k* is usually pronounced [ŋ].
>
>   EXAMPLES: kings   hungry   single   thank   drink

EXERCISE B

Read the following phrases and sentences aloud carefully. The boldface words should be pronounced with [ŋ]. *(Remember—back of the tongue must go up toward the palate).* **This exercise is not on the tape.**

1. Good **evening**.
2. I'm **going** home.
3. Is **something wrong**?
4. **ring** on my **finger**
5. **raining** and **snowing**
6. Are you **coming along**?
7. The **singer sang** the **song**.
8. Mrs. **King** is **doing** the **washing**.
9. I **think** the **young** boy is **winning**.
10. We are **studying reading** and **writing**.

Read the following words aloud. Circle only the words that are pronounced with [ŋ]. **This self-test is not on the tape.**

(1. bring)	6. tangerine	11. along	16. engage
2. anger	7. swing	12. talking	17. stinging
3. hang	8. tangle	13. sponge	18. stingy
4. angel	9. danger	14. grin	19. lunch
5. dancing	10. sink	15. running	20. bank

FOR AN ENCORE . . . .

READING

Find three employment advertisements in the newspaper classified section. Circle all [ŋ] words. Practice reading the ads out loud producing all [ŋ] words accurately.

《《**JUST KEEP STUDYING, THINKING, AND PRACTICING,**

EVERYTHING WILL BE OK WITH [ŋ]!!!》》

REVIEW ROUNDUP
[k]   [g]   [m]   [n]   [ŋ]

REVIEW EXERCISE

Repeat the rows of words and sentences accurately after your teacher or the instructor on the tape. Feel the movement from the **lips** to **tongue tip** to **back of the throat** as you pronounce [m], [n], [ŋ], [k], [g].

[m]	[n]	[ŋ]	[k]	[g]
1. whi**m**	wi**n**	wi**ng**	wi**ck**	wi**g**
2. ba**m**	ba**n**	ba**ng**	ba**ck**	ba**g**
3. ta**m**	ta**n**	ta**ng**	ta**ck**	ta**g**
4. ra**m**	ra**n**	ra**ng**	ra**ck**	ra**g**

5. **Bing** has a **big ring**.
      [ŋ]   [g] [ŋ]

6. My **son sang some songs**.
          [n]   [ŋ]   [m]   [ŋ]

7. **Tim thinks** that **thing** is **thick**.
     [m]   [ŋ]   [ŋ]   [k]

8. **Kim** is **kin** to the **king**.
     [m]   [n]   [ŋ]

9. **Sam's sack** is **sagging**.
     [m]   [k]   [g] [ŋ]

10. I **seem** to have **seen** him **sing**.
       [m]   [n]   [ŋ]

REVIEW TEST I
(Correct answers may be found in Appendix II on p. 285.)

Read the following sentences aloud; choose the correct word to complete the sentence. Be sure to pronounce each nasal consonant carefully. **This review test is not on the tape.**

Pronunciation Hints: [m] = lips together
[n] = tongue tip to upper gum ridge
[ŋ] = back of tongue up to soft palate

1. Jean sat in the _____   (sum   sun   sung)
2. The bird hurt its _____   (whim   win   wing)
3. It is fun to _____   (rum   run   rung)
4. The meat needs to_____   (simmer   sinner   singer)
5. They removed the_____   (bam   ban   band)

REVIEW TEST II
(Correct answers may be found in Appendix II on p. 285.)

Your teacher or the instructor on the tape will present the following sentences using ONLY ONE of the choices. Listen carefully and circle the word and consonant used.

EXAMPLE: Give me the (cone   comb).
[n]   [m]

1. I'll call (them   then).
[m]   [n]

2. He (ran   rang) twice.
[n]   [ŋ]

3. That (bun   bum) is old.
[n]   [m]

4. We got (some   sun) at the beach.
[m]   [n]

5. It's an old (rag   rack).
[g]   [k]

After checking your answers in Appendix II, read each of the sentences twice. Use the first word in the first reading and the contrast word in the second reading.

REVIEW TEST III (Correct answers may be found in Appendix II on p. 286.)

Read the following "commercial" aloud. In the brackets provided, write the phonetic symbol representing the sound of the underlined letters. **This review test is not on the tape.**

Pronunciation Key: [m] as in **me**   [k] as in **cake**
[n] as in **no**   [g] as in **go**
[ŋ] as in **ring**

. . . .

ANNOUNCER:

        [n]   [ŋ]   [ ] [ ]   [ ]
Is your skin feeling dry? Are you finding new wrinkles,
[ ]   [ ]   [ ]   [ ] [ ]   [ ]
bags, and lines? Then you need Pom's Skin Cream. Men
      [ ]   [ ]   [ ]
and women everywhere brag about our cream. Listen to
      [ ]   [ ]   [ ]   [ ]
famous film star Molly Malone who has been acting for a
[ ] [ ] [ ]
long, long, long time.

MOLLY:

                            [ ][ ]
Hmmmmmm. Of course, everyone knows I started mak-
[ ] [ ]   [ ]   [ ]   [ ]
ing films when I was nine. But I've been using Pom's
                [ ]   [ ]
Cream for years and I think it's wonderful. Just put it on
      [ ]   [ ]   [ ]   [ ]
every morning and evening and in one week you'll start
[ ]   [ ]   [ ]   [ ]
seeing a big difference. Your face will gleam and shine
       [ ]   [ ]
and you'll look just fine!

ANNOUNCER:

              [ ]   [ ]   [ ][ ]
And now for a limited time, you can get two jars for the
     [ ]   [ ]   [ ]   [ ]   [ ]
price of one. Remember, use Pom's Skin Cream and
   [ ]   [ ]
you too can look like a film star!

Review [k] [g] pm] [n] [ŋ] **119**

PRONOUNCING FINAL CONSONANTS

FINAL CONSONANTS IN ENGLISH

A final consonant is any consonant that is the last sound in a word. Consonant sounds that end words are *very* important. They can determine grammatical as well as word meaning. Careful production of final consonants is necessary to convey your message correctly and to sound like a native English speaker.

NOTE: Words pronounced with a final consonant often have "*e*" as the final letter. When "*e*" is the last letter in a word, it is usually silent; a consonant is actually the last SOUND.

EXAMPLES: ma**d**e   pho**n**e   bi**t**e   ha**v**e

POSSIBLE PRONUNCIATION PROBLEMS

In your language, consonants rarely end words. However, in English, most words end in consonants. Because you are not accustomed to saying final consonants, you frequently omit them in English or add a vowel sound to the end of the word. Without realizing it, you can confuse your listeners; they might not understand you.

EXAMPLE A: You will not be saying your target word.

> **place** will sound like **play**
> **forth** will sound like **four**

EXAMPLE B: Your speech will be difficult to understand.

> **hat**   will sound like **hato**
> **dog**   will sound like **dogu**
> **some** will sound like **soma**

The words in each of the following rows will sound the same if their final consonant is omitted. Repeat each row after your teacher or the instructor on the tape. Carefully pronounce the final consonant in each word without adding a vowel sound to the end.

1. cat	cap	can	cab
2. soon	soup	suit	sued
3. ten	tense	tent	tend
4. sight	side	sign	size
5. car	cart	card	carp

EXERCISE B

Read the following word combinations aloud. Carefully distinguish between them by exaggerated pronunciation of the final consonants. **This exercise is not on the tape.**

1. I saw	eye sore	I sawed
2. Joe knows her	Joan owes her	Joan knows her
3. heat wave	he waved	he waves
4. I'll earn it	I learn it	I earn it
5. I sigh	eye sight	I sighed

EXERCISE C

Read the following word pairs aloud. Be sure to keep your vocal cords vibrating as you pronounce the final consonants of the words in the second column. **This exercise is not on the tape.**

Voiceless Final Consonant	Voiced Final Consonant
ha**t**	ha**d**
sigh**t**	si**de**
mo**p**	mo**b**
ro**pe**	ro**be**
ra**ck**	ra**g**
bu**s**	bu**zz**
hal**f**	ha**ve**

EXERCISE D

Read the following sentences aloud. Carefully pronounce the final consonant in each boldface word. **This exercise is not on the tape.**

1. She **sighed** at the beautiful **sight**.
2. **Bess** is the **best** artist.
3. **Can't** Amy **catch** a **cab**?
4. The thief **stole** the **stove**.
5. **Ben** couldn't **bend** his knees.
6. The **coal** is very **cold**.
7. We **paid** for the **pane** of glass.
8. **I'm** sure **I'll** go.
9. **Would** he like a **wool** coat?
10. She **sat** on the **sack** full of **sap**.

EXERCISE E

Read the following dialogue aloud. Be sure to carefully pronounce the final consonant sound in each boldface word. **This exercise is not on the tape.**

••

PATRICK: Hi, **Pam**. **Have** you **had** dinner at the **Old Inn**?
PAM: No, **Pat**. But **Bea** said their **beef** can't be **beat**.
PATRICK: And **Hal** told me to **have** the **ham**.
PAM: **Doug** said the **duck** was **done** just right.
PATRICK: And **Sue** thought the **soup** would **suit** a king!
PAM: **Kate raved** about the **cake**.
PATRICK: I'd say the **inn** was **it**! **Pam**, will you be ready at **eight**?
PAM: Oh, **Pat**, I already am! I thought you'd never **ask**!

••

The exciting story of **Pam** and **Pat** at the **Old Inn** continues in Self-Test III.

 # SELF-TEST I   (Correct answers may be found in Appendix II on p. 287.)

Your teacher or the instructor on the tape will present ten three-word series. Write the numbers 1, 2, or 3 on the line above each word to correspond with the order of word presentation. **Listen carefully** for the final consonant sound in each word.

EXAMPLE: The instructor says: *half*   *hat*   *had*
                                                        2   3   1
                          You write: hat   had   half

1. hot   hog   hop

2. pat   pack   pan

3. save   safe   same

4. big   bid   bib

5. cake   came   cane

6. mad   mat   map

7. fade   fate   fake

8. wipe   white   wife

9. peg   pen   pet

10. hike   hide   height

SELF-TEST II   (Correct answers may be found in Appendix II on p. 287.)

Read the following sentences aloud. Carefully pronounce the final consonant sound of each word you choose to fill in the blanks. **This self-test is
not on the tape.**

1. Wash your hands with _____.   (soak soap sewn)
2. _____ the dirty dishes.   (soak soap sewn)
3. Can you read that _____?   (sign sight size)
4. Do the socks come in my _____?   (sign sight size)
5. I like _____ and eggs.   (hat ham half)
6. Be home by _____ past five.   (hat ham half)
7. The _____ of the perfume is strong.   (send scent cents)
8. A dime is worth ten _____.   (send scent cents)
9. Make a birthday _____.   (whip wish with)
10. _____ the cream well.   (whip wish with)

SELF-TEST III   (Correct answers may be found in Appendix II on p. 288.)

Read the following dialogue aloud. Fill in the blanks with the final consonant sound that completes the word. **This self-test is not on the tape.**

....

ANN: Hi, Pam! How was your da_e last nigh_ with Pat?
PAM: Nothing went righ_ last nigh_. Pa_ had a fla_ tire and came la_e!
ANN: How was the foo_ at the Ol_ Inn?
PAM: It was ba_. The soup was col_. My stea_ was tough. They ran out of chocola_e ca_e.
ANN: What about the dinner Pa_ a_e?
PAM: His duc_ was overdo_e. His garli_ brea_ was sta_e!
ANN: Did it cos_ a lot of money?
PAM: Yes! And Pat didn't ha_e enough to pay the bi__.
ANN: I guess you won'_ go ou_ with him agai_!
PAM: Why do you say tha_? We're going for a bike ri_e this afternoon. He's so handso_e!

....

After checking your answers in Appendix II, practice this dialogue again. Carefully pronounce all final consonant sounds.

FOR AN ENCORE . . . .

CONVERSATION

Tape-record yourself while talking on the telephone. After you hang up, play back the recording. Analyze your speech and listen for final consonants. Make a list of words you didn't pronounce carefully and practice them.

PRONOUNCING PAST TENSE VERBS

When writing English, we add the ending -ed to form the past tense of regular verbs. That's easy to remember! However, when *speaking* English, the -ed ending can have three different pronunciations. Sometimes -ed sounds like **[t]**, as in *stopped* [stapt]; sometimes it sounds like **[d]**, as in *lived* [lɪvd]; sometimes it sounds like a new syllable, **[ɪd]**, as in *loaded* [loʊdɪd].*

POSSIBLE PRONUNCIATION PROBLEMS

As discussed in the chapter on final consonant sounds (page 120), most consonant sounds do not end words in your language. Consequently, you are not used to saying final consonants in English. This might make you omit or mispronounce past tense verb endings.

EXAMPLE A: Past tense verbs will sound like present tense verbs:

> **washed** will sound like **wash**
> **played** will sound like **play**

EXAMPLE B: A new syllable will be incorrectly added to a past tense verb:

> **lived**   [lɪvd] will sound like **live-id** [lɪvɪd]
> **tapped** [tæpt] will sound like **tap-id** [tæpɪd]

EXAMPLE C: You will not be saying your target past tense verb:

> **played** [pleɪd] will sound like **plate** [pleɪt]
> **tied**   [taɪd] will sound like **tight** [taɪt]

This might seem confusing *but don't worry! WE HAVE GOOD NEWS!* In this chapter we will teach you three **EASY** rules to help you pronounce past tense regular verbs correctly. You will learn when -ed sounds like [t], [d], or [ɪd]. Study the rules and *you've got it made!*

*Refer to a key to Pronouncing the Vowels of American English on page 139.

-ed PRONOUNCED [t]

The ending -ed will always sound like [t] when the last sound in the present tense verb* is voiceless.†

EXAMPLES: talked [tɔkt]   crossed [krɔst]   laughed [læft]

 ## EXERCISE A

Repeat the following verbs after your teacher or the instructor on the tape. Be sure to pronounce the -ed in the past tense verbs like [t]. (Do NOT add a new syllable to any word!)

Present Tense Verbs	Past Tense Verbs
(Last sound is voiceless)	**(-ed = [t])**
1. look	looked
2. miss	missed
3. stop	stopped
4. work	worked
5. pick	picked

-ed PRONOUNCED [d]

The ending -ed will always sound like [d] when the last sound in the present tense verb is a vowel or voiced consonant.

EXAMPLES: lived [lɪvd]   turned [tɝnd]   played [pleɪd]

---

*Rules apply to *regular* past tense verbs.

†Refer to page 9 for a review of voiceless and voiced sounds.

EXERCISE B

Repeat the following verbs after your teacher or the instructor on the tape. Be sure to pronounce -ed like [d]. (Do NOT add a new syllable to the words!)

Present Tense Verbs	Past Tense Verbs
(Last sound is voiced)	**(-ed = [d])**
1. love	loved
2. stay	stayed
3. fill	filled
4. burn	burned
5. rain	rained

-ed PRONOUNCED [ɪd]

The ending -ed will always sound like the new syllable [ɪd] when the last sound in the present tense verb is [t] or [d].

EXAMPLES: want<u>ed</u> [wantɪd]   rest<u>ed</u> [rɛstɪd]   end<u>ed</u> [ɛndɪd]

EXERCISE C

Repeat the following verbs after your teacher or the instructor on the tape. **NOW** you should pronounce -ed like the new syllable [ɪd]!

Present Tense Verbs	Past Tense Verbs
(End in *t* or *d*)	**(-ed = the new syllable [ɪd])**
1. end	ended
2. add	added
3. hunt	hunted
4. want	wanted
5. need	needed

EXERCISE D

Read the following sentences aloud. Be sure to pronounce the -ed ending in the past tense verbs correctly. **This exercise is not on the tape.**

-ed = [t]	-ed = [d]	-ed = [ɪd]
She cooked dinner.	We played a game.	He avoided his boss.
The boy danced all night.	He moved again.	I rested at home.
The bus stopped in the road.	Ted stayed out late.	The car started.
Mom baked a pie.	I mailed a letter.	Mike needed money.
She finished early.	We opened a window.	Our house was painted.

Sue packed her suitcase and waited for a taxi.
      [t]   [ɪd]

Tim cashed a check and deposited the money.
      [t]   [ɪd]

The children played games and jumped rope.
          [d]   [t]

I studied hard but failed the test.
    [d]   [d]

He listened while I showed photos and talked about my trip.
      [d]   [d]   [t]

SELF-TEST I   (Correct answers may be found in Appendix II on p. 288.)

Read the sentences on page 130 aloud. Choose the correct past tense verb from the list to fill in the blanks. In the brackets, write either [t], [d], or [ɪd] to represent the -ed sound in the verb. **This self-test is not on the tape.**

painted	mailed	danced	washed	waited
lived	deposited	asked	walked	talked

EXAMPLE: I <u>locked</u> the door. [t]

1. We _____ the rumba and tango. [ ]
2. She _____ on the phone for an hour. [ ]
3. Dad _____ the fence green. [ ]
4. The student _____ three questions. [ ]
5. They _____ 15 minutes for the bus. [ ]
6. I've _____ in the same house for four years. [ ]
7. My father _____ a letter. [ ]
8. The man _____ five miles. [ ]
9. I _____ my check in the bank. [ ]
10. He _____ his car with a hose. [ ]

SELF-TEST II   (Correct answers may be found in Appendix II on p. 288.)

Repeat each three-word series after your teacher or the instructor on the tape. Circle the ONE word in each group that has a different -ed sound than the others.

EXAMPLE: (placed)   pleased   played

1.	stopped	started	stated
2.	finished	followed	phoned
3.	loved	looked	liked
4.	tasted	traded	tapped
5.	cooked	cleaned	baked
6.	packed	pasted	passed
7.	ironed	sewed	mended
8.	whispered	shouted	screamed
9.	skipped	hopped	lifted
10.	pushed	pulled	raised

SELF-TEST III

(Correct answers may be found in Appendix II on p. 289.)

Read the following dialogue aloud. In the brackets above each past tense verb, write the phonetic symbol representing the sound of the *-ed* ending. **This self-test is not on the tape.**

....

                                     [ɪd]
ROBERTA: Kate, have you started your diet? I hope you haven't
               [d]
              gained any weight.
              [ ]   [ ]
KATE: I boiled eggs and sliced celery for lunch.
                  [ ]
ROBERTA: Have you exercised at all?
             [ ]   [ ]
KATE: I walked five miles and jogged in the park.
                [ ]   [ ]
ROBERTA: Have you cleaned the house? Calories can be worked off!
             [ ]   [ ]   [ ]
KATE: I washed and waxed the floors. I even painted the bathroom.
             [ ]   [ ]
ROBERTA: Who baked this apple pie? Who cooked this ham?
                [ ]   [ ]   [ ]
KATE: When I finished cleaning I was starved. I prepared this food
             for dinner.
                                         [ ]
ROBERTA: Oh, no! I'll take this food home so you won't be tempted.
               [ ]
             I really enjoyed being with you. Your diet is great!
             [ ]   [ ]
KATE: What happened? Somehow, I missed out on all the fun.

....

After checking your answers in Appendix II, read this dialogue aloud with a friend. Be sure to pronounce all past tense endings correctly.

PRONOUNCING PLURALS, THIRD-PERSON VERBS, POSSESSIVES, AND CONTRACTIONS

When writing English, the letter *s* at the end of words serves many different purposes. *S* is used to form plural nouns (hat**s**, dog**s**); third-person present tense regular verbs (he like**s**; she eat**s**); possessive nouns (my friend'**s** house; the dog'**s** collar); and contractions (it'**s** late; he'**s** here). As you can see, *s* is a very versatile letter in English. It is important to learn its many different "sounds"!

When speaking English, the -*s* ending can have three different pronunciations. It can sound like **[s]**, as in *hats* [hæts]; **[z]** as in *tells* [tɛlz]; or as the new syllable **[ɪz]**, as in *roses* [roʊzɪz].

POSSIBLE PRONUNCIATION PROBLEMS

Your possible tendency to drop final consonants results in omissions or incorrect pronunciations of -*s* at the ends of words. This will make you difficult to understand and confuse your listeners.

EXAMPLE A: Plural nouns will sound like singular nouns:

> **Two books** will sound like **two book**.

EXAMPLE B: Third-person present tense verbs will be incorrect:

> **He eats**   will sound like **he eat**.
> **She sings** will sound like **she sing**.

EXAMPLE C: Possessives and contractions will be omitted:

> **Bob's house** will sound like **Bob house**.
> **He's right**   will sound like **he right**.

-S PRONOUNCED [z]

The -s forming the plural always sounds like [s] when the last sound in the singular noun is voiceless.

EXAMPLES: *hats* [hæts]   *lips* [lɪps]   *sticks* [stɪks]

The -s forming the third-person present always sounds like [s] when the last sound in the verb infinitive is voiceless.

EXAMPLES: *he likes* [laɪks].   *she talks* [tɔks].   *it floats* [flouts].

The -s forming the possessive always sounds like [s] when the last sound in the noun is voiceless.

EXAMPLES: *Pat's* [pæts] *car*   *the book's* [bʊks] *binding*

The -s forming the contractions always sounds like [s] when the last sound in the word being contracted is voiceless.

EXAMPLES: *It's* [ɪts] *true.*   *That's* [ðæts] *my house.*

 # EXERCISE A

Repeat the following phrases after your teacher or the instructor on the tape. The final -s will sound like [s]. (Do NOT add a new syllable to any word!)

Plural Noun Phrases	Third-Person Verb Phrases	Possessive/Contraction Phrases
Bake the cakes.	He smokes too much.	the cat's milk
Wash the plates.	She sleeps late.	Ralph's friend
Stack the cups.	It tastes good.	the plant's leaves
Clean the pots.	My mother makes tea.	Let's eat now.
Darn the socks.	The dog eats.	What's wrong?

-S PRONOUNCED [z]

The -s forming the plural always sounds like [z] when the last sound in the singular noun is voiced.

EXAMPLES: floors [flɔrz]   bags [bægz]   cars [kɑrz]

The -s forming the third-person present always sounds like [z] when the last sound in the verb infinitive is voiced.

EXAMPLES: He swims [swɪmz].   The bird flies [flaɪz].   She sings [sɪŋz].

The -s forming the possessive always sounds like [z] when the last sound in the noun is voiced.

EXAMPLES: Tim's [tɪmz] house   my friend's [frɛndz] cat

The -s forming a contraction always sounds like [z] when the last sound in the word being contracted is voiced.

EXAMPLES: She's [ʃiz] my sister.   He's [hiz] leaving.

EXERCISE B

Repeat the following phrases after your teacher or the instructor on the tape. Remember, the -s ending must sound like [z].

Plural Noun Phrases	Third-Person Verb Phrases	Possessive/Contraction Phrases
Close your eyes.	He saves money.	Sue's pencil
Kill the fleas.	The man lives here.	the baby's milk
Sing the songs.	Dad reads books.	our teacher's desk
lost 30 pounds	The boy listens.	my friend's house
Open the letters.	It smells good.	Here's a pencil.

-S (or -es) PRONOUNCED [ɪz]

The -s or -es forming the plural always sounds like the new syllable [ɪz] when the last sound in the singular noun is [s], [z], [ʃ], [tʃ], [dʒ], or [ʒ].

EXAMPLES: wish<u>es</u> [wɪʃɪz]   church<u>es</u> [tʃɝtʃɪz]   places [pleɪsɪz]

The -s or -es forming the third-person present always sounds like the new syllable [ɪz] when the last sound in the verb infinitive is [s], [z], [ʃ], [tʃ], [dʒ], or [ʒ].

EXAMPLES: He watch<u>es</u> [watʃɪz].   The bee buzz<u>es</u> [bʌzɪz].

The -s or -es forming the possessive always sounds like the new syllable [ɪz] when the last sound in the noun is [s], [z], [ʃ], [tʃ], [dʒ] or [ʒ].

EXAMPLES: the rose'<u>s</u> [rouzɪz] stem   the church'<u>s</u> [tʃɝtʃɪz] altar

EXERCISE C

Repeat the following phrases after your teacher or the instructor on the tape. **Now** you should pronounce **s** like the new syllable [ɪz]!

Plural Noun Phrases	Third-Person Verb Phrases	Possessive Phrases
two new dresses	He wishes.	the church's steeple
Trim the hedges.	She watches him.	the witch's broom
Buy the watches.	He judges the contest.	Mr. Jones's pen
Win the prizes.	Mother washes clothes.	the mouse's cheese
in the cages	The bee buzzes.	the bus's tires

EXERCISE D

Read the following sentences aloud. Be sure to pronounce the *s* ending in the plurals, verbs, possessives, and contractions correctly. **This exercise is not on the tape.**

s = [s]	s = [z]	s = [ɪz]
He wants to leave.	Blow out the candles.	The speeches are boring.
My sister likes gum.	The hen laid eggs.	Please turn the pages.
I read many books.	Guns are dangerous.	Mary dances well.
Mother ironed shirts.	Here's some money.	I won many prizes.
Jack's not coming.	The girl's dress is old.	You have three choices.

Boys play cowboys and Indians and use toy guns and knives.
  [z]   [z]   [z]   [z]   [z]

The store sells watches, rings, bracelets, diamonds, and rubies.
        [z]   [ɪz]   [z]   [s]   [z]   [z]

My sister's dresses, blouses, and shoes are new.
    [z]   [ɪz]   [ɪz]   [z]

Our teacher's favorite saying is "Where there's a will, there's a way."
    [z]   [z]   [z]

Tim's friend's house has lots of rooms with oriental carpets.
[z]   [z]   [s]   [z]   [s]

Repeat each three-word series after your teacher or the instructor on the tape. Circle the ONE word in each group of three that has a different -s ending sound than the others.

EXAMPLE:	belts	hats	(ties)
1.	talks	walks	runs
2.	dishes	gates	pages
3.	pears	apples	oranges
4.	eyes	noses	toes
5.	saves	makes	cooks
6.	newspapers	magazines	books
7.	dogs	birds	cats
8.	tables	chairs	couches
9.	dentists	doctors	lawyers
10.	lunches	beaches	chimes

SELF-TEST II (Correct answers may be found in Appendix II on p. 290.)

Read the dialogue on page 138 aloud. In the brackets below each under-lined -s, write the phonetic symbol representing the sound of that -s ending. **This self-test is not on the tape.**

CHARLES: Hi, James, What's new?
　　　　　[z]　　[s]

JAMES: Nothing, Charles. All the guys have dates for the prom except me!
　　　　[z]　　　　[z]　　　[s]

CHARLES: That's all right. You can take Bess's sister Nancy.
　　　　　[ ]　　　　　　　　　　　　　[ ]

JAMES: What's she like?
　　　　[ ]

CHARLES: She measures about 5 feet 2 inches, has blue eyes, and
　　　　　　　　[ ]　　　　　　　　　　[ ]　　　　[ ]
　　　　　weighs 102 pounds. She looks like a model.
　　　　　　[ ]　　　　[ ]　　　　[ ]

JAMES: Then she probably dislikes her studies.
　　　　　　　　　　　　　　[ ]　　　[ ]

CHARLES: That's not true. She enters law school after finals. She's on the
　　　　　[ ]　　　　　　　[ ]　　　　　　　　　　[ ]　　[ ]
　　　　　Dean's List.*
　　　　　　[ ]

JAMES: What are her hobbies? She probably hates sports!
　　　　　　　　　　[ ]　　　　　　　[ ]　　[ ]

CHARLES: She golfs, plays tennis, and swims. She also dances very well.
　　　　　　[ ]　　[ ]　　　　　　[ ]　　　　　　[ ]

JAMES: There's got to be SOMETHING wrong! She probably has no
　　　　　[ ]
　　　　dates.
　　　　　[ ]

CHARLES: She has lots of boyfriends. In fact, let's make some changes. I'll
　　　　　　　　[ ]　　　[ ]　　　　[ ]　　　　　　　　　[ ]
　　　　　take Bess's sister! You can take Mary.
　　　　　　　[ ]

JAMES: NO WAY! There will be no exchanges! Nancy sounds great. I
　　　　　　　　　　　　　　　　[ ]　　　　　[ ]
　　　　just hope she likes me!
　　　　　　　　[ ]

*Dean's List = an honor roll for very intelligent students.

138 PLURALS, THIRD-PERSON VERBS, POSSESSIVES, CONTRACTIONS

A KEY TO PRONOUNCING THE VOWELS OF AMERICAN ENGLISH

You have probably discovered that there is a big difference between the way words are spelled in English and the way they are pronounced. English spelling patterns are inconsistent and are not always a reliable guide to pronunciation. For example, in the following words, the letter *a* is used to represent five different sounds.

h**a**te   f**a**ther   h**a**ve   **a**ny   s**a**w

Pretty confusing, right? That's why we need a set of symbols in which *each* sound is represented by a *different* symbol. In this program, you will learn the International Phonetic Alphabet (IPA), which is used all over the world. It consists of a set of symbols in which **ONE SYMBOL** always represents **ONE SOUND**.

DON'T PANIC! It is not necessary to learn all of the symbols at once. Each sound will be introduced and explained **one at a time**. You will learn the symbols easily as you progress through the book. A pronunciation key* to the different vowels and diphthongs of American English with their IPA and dictionary symbols is presented on the next page. Refer to it often for review.

To help you learn the exact pronunciation of the phonetic symbols and key words, the Key to Pronouncing the Vowels of American English has been recorded at the beginning of Tape 2, Side A. You will hear each phonetic symbol introduced and pronounced once. Each English key word will be said once. Listen carefully to this first recording **before** continuing with the program.

A KEY TO PRONOUNCING THE VOWELS OF AMERICAN ENGLISH

INTERNATIONAL PHONETIC ALPHABET SYMBOL	DICTIONARY SYMBOL	ENGLISH KEY WORDS
SECTION ONE		
[i]	ē	m<u>e</u>, t<u>ea</u>, b<u>ee</u>
[ɪ]	i or ĭ	<u>i</u>t, p<u>i</u>n
[eɪ]	ā	<u>a</u>te, g<u>a</u>me, th<u>ey</u>
[ɛ]	e or ĕ	<u>e</u>gg, h<u>ea</u>d, p<u>e</u>t
[æ]	a or ă	<u>a</u>t, f<u>a</u>t, h<u>a</u>ppy
[a]	ä or ŏ	h<u>o</u>t, f<u>a</u>ther
SECTION TWO		
[u]	o͞o	y<u>ou</u>, t<u>oo</u>, r<u>u</u>le
[ʊ]	oo or o͝o	p<u>u</u>t, c<u>oo</u>k
[ʌ]	u or ŭ	<u>u</u>p, b<u>u</u>t, c<u>o</u>me
[ou]	ō	b<u>oa</u>t, n<u>o</u>, <u>o</u>h
[ɔ]	ô	<u>a</u>ll, b<u>o</u>ss, c<u>au</u>ght
SECTION THREE		
[ə]	ə	sod<u>a</u>, <u>u</u>pon
[ɝ]	ûr	<u>ur</u>n, f<u>ir</u>st, s<u>er</u>ve
[ɚ]	ər	fath<u>er</u>, aft<u>er</u>
[aʊ]	ou	<u>ou</u>t, c<u>ow</u>, h<u>ou</u>se
[aɪ]	ī	m<u>y</u>, p<u>ie</u>, <u>I</u>
[ɔɪ]	oi	<u>oi</u>l, b<u>oy</u>, n<u>oi</u>se

*The pronunciation taught is that of "general American" speech which is used by most American English speakers.

Definitions

As you progress through this manual, you will frequently see the terms *vowels*, *diphthongs*, and *articulators*. We will now define these terms for you.

VOWEL: A vowel is a speech sound produced with vibrating vocal cords and a continuous unrestricted flow of air coming from the mouth. The most well-known vowels in English are

A   E   I   O   and   **U.**

DIPHTHONG: A diphthong is a combination of two vowel sounds. It begins as one vowel and ends as another. During the production of a diphthong, your articulators glide from the position of the first vowel to the position of the second. For example, when pronouncing [eɪ] as in "vein," your articulators glide from the vowel [e] to the vowel [ɪ].

In English, the most common diphthongs are [aʊ], [eɪ], [aɪ], [ɔɪ] and [oʊ].

ARTICULATORS: The articulators are the different parts of the mouth area that we use when speaking, such as the lips, tongue, teeth, and jaw.

The various vowel sounds are affected by the changing shape and position of your articulators. The different vowels are created by:

A. **The position of your tongue in the mouth.** For example, the tongue is high in the mouth for the vowel [i] as in "see," but is low in the mouth for the vowel [a] as in "hot."

B. **The shape of your lips.** For example, the lips are very rounded for the vowel [u] as in "new," but are spread for [i] as in "see."

C. **The size of your jaw opening.** For example, the jaw is open much wider for [a] as in "hot" than it is for the diphthong [eɪ] as in "pay."

PRONOUNCING VOWELS

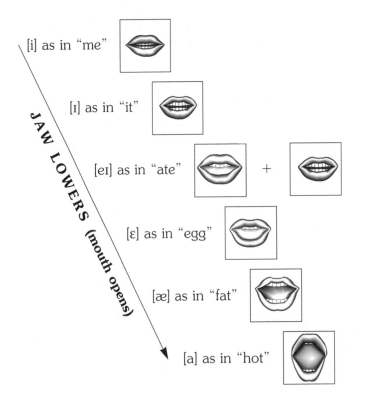

[i] as in "me"

[ɪ] as in "it"

JAW LOWERS (mouth opens)

[eɪ] as in "ate"   +

[ɛ] as in "egg"

[æ] as in "fat"

[a] as in "hot"

You can see in the pictures how the jaw moves from a closed position to an open one during pronunciation of the vowel sequence [i] [ɪ] [eɪ] [ɛ] [æ] [a]. Becoming familiar with this progression and understanding the relationship of one vowel to another will help you with your pronunciation of the vowels.

EXAMPLES: The phonetic symbol [ɪ] represents a sound between [i] and [eɪ]. It is pronounced with the jaw and tongue raised more than for [eɪ], but not as much as for [i].

The symbol [æ] represents a sound between [ɛ] and [a]. [æ] is pronounced with the jaw open more than for [ɛ], but not as much as for [a].

This may seem a bit confusing at first. Refer to these pictures whenever you have difficulty pronouncing any of the vowels. Repeat the sequence [i] [ɪ] [eɪ] [ɛ] [æ] [a] several times. Be sure to see and feel the progressive dropping of your tongue and jaw as you pronounce each sound.

PRONOUNCING VOWELS

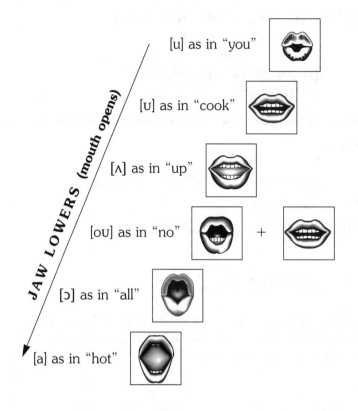

[u] as in "you"

[ʊ] as in "cook"

[ʌ] as in "up"

[oʊ] as in "no"   +

[ɔ] as in "all"

[a] as in "hot"

JAW LOWERS (mouth opens)

Once again you can see how the jaw moves from a closed position to an open one during the pronunciation of a vowel sequence. Practice pronouncing the series several times. Place your hand under your chin and feel your jaw drop with the pronunciation of each vowel.

Refer to these pictures whenever you are confused about the pronunciation of any of the vowels. Repeat the sequence [u] [ʊ] [ʌ] [oʊ] [ɔ] [a] several times. You'll be able to see and feel your jaw lower as you pronounce the vowels in the series. **TRY IT NOW! IT REALLY WORKS!!!**

[i] as in *ME, TEA,* and *BEE*
(DICTIONARY MARK: ē)
and
[ɪ] as in *IT* and *PIN*
(DICTIONARY MARK: i or ĭ)

PRONOUNCING [i]

LIPS: are tense and in a "smile" position.

JAW: is completely raised.

TONGUE: is high near the roof of the mouth.

POSSIBLE PRONUNCIATION PROBLEMS

Pronunciation problems occur because of confusing English spelling patterns and the similarity of [i] and [ɪ] (the sound to be described next). It's easy to understand why some speakers are afraid to say words like "sheet" or "beach!"

EXAMPLES: When you substitute [ɪ] for [i]: **sheep** becomes **ship**.
eat becomes **it**.

Remember to feel tension in your lips, tongue, and jaw. **[i]** is a LONG sound; be sure to prolong it. **SMILE when you say [i]**; **W̲E̲ GUARANTEE it's E̲ASY to say [i]!**

The following words should all be pronounced with [i]. Repeat them carefully after your teacher or the instructor on the tape.

[i] At the Beginning	[i] In the Middle	[i] At the End
eat	mean	he
eel	need	bee
east	keen	key
easy	deep	tea
each	scene	fee

[i] spelled:

"e"	"ee"	"ea"	"ie" or "ei"
he	see	east	niece
we	eel	lean	brief
me	deed	team	piece
scene	heel	cheap	belief
these	needy	peach	either

Less frequent spelling patterns for [i] consist of the letters *i* and *eo*.

EXAMPLES: police   people

HINTS: a. The letters *ee* are usually pronounced [i].

EXAMPLES: see   green   feet   freedom

b. The letters *ei* and *ie* are usually pronounced [i].

EXAMPLES: either   receive   piece   grief

NOTE: **When speaking English, international students frequently forget to prolong the [i] vowel before consonants.**

EXERCISE B

Read the following pairs of [i] words aloud. PROLONG the [i] vowel before the consonant. (The dots are there to remind you to lengthen the [i].) **This exercise is not on the tape.**

1. fee   fee ....d   (feed)
2. see   see ....d   (seed)
3. pea   pea ....s   (peas)
4. bee   bee........s   (bees)
5. tea   tea ....m   (team)

 ## EXERCISE C

The boldface words in the following phrases and sentences should all be pronounced with the vowel [i]. Repeat them carefully after your teacher or the instructor on the tape.

1. **See** you next **week**.
2. **See** you this **evening**.
3. **See** you at **three**.
4. **See** what I **mean**?
5. **Pleased** to **meet** you.
6. **Steve eats cream cheese**.
7. **Lee** has a **reason** for **leaving**.
8. **She received** her **teaching degree**.
9. A friend in **need**, is a friend **indeed**!
10. They **reached** a **peace agreement**.

Read each series of four words out loud. Circle the **ONE** word in each group of four that is **NOT** pronounced with [i]. **This self-test is not on the tape.**

EXAMPLES: keep   lean   (fit)   piece

1. bead   great   leave   tea
2. eight   either   believe   niece
3. scene   women   these   even
4. need   been   sleep   thirteen
5. police   thief   machine   vision
6. pretty   wheat   sweet   cream
7. people   bread   deal   east
8. tin   teen   steam   receive
9. leave   live   leaf   lease
10. steep   Steve   easy   still

PRONOUNCING [ɪ]

LIPS: **are relaxed and slightly parted.**

JAW: **is slightly lower than for [i].**

TONGUE: is high, but lower than for [i].

POSSIBLE PRONUNCIATION PROBLEMS

The vowel [ɪ] does not exist in many languages and may be difficult for you to recognize and say. You probably substitute the more familiar [i] sound.

EXAMPLES: When you substitute [i] for [ɪ]:   **hit** becomes **heat**.
                                                itch becomes **each**.

As you practice the exercises, remember NOT to "smile" and tense your lips as you would for [i]. [ɪ] **is a SHORT, QUICK sound; your lips should barely move as you say it.**

The following words should all be pronounced with [ɪ]. Repeat them carefully after your teacher or the instructor on the tape.

[ɪ] At the Beginning

is
if
it
ill
itch

[ɪ] In the Middle

pin
lift
give
miss
listen

[ɪ] spelled:

"y"	"ui"	"i"
gym	build	sin
syrup	quick	lips
symbol	quilt	with
system	guilty	gift
rhythm	guitar	differ

Less frequent spelling patterns for [ɪ] consist of the letters *o, e, u,* and *ee.*

EXAMPLES: w**o**men   pr**e**tty   b**u**sy   b**ee**n

> **HINT:**   The most common spelling pattern for [ɪ] is the letter *i* followed by a final consonant.
>
> EXAMPLES: w**in**   th**is**   h**it**   tr**ip**   beg**in**

EXERCISE B

The boldface words in the following phrases and sentences should all be pronounced with the [ɪ] vowel. Repeat them carefully after your teacher or the instructor on the tape.

1. **This is it**.
2. What **is this**?
3. **This is** my **sister**.
4. **This is Miss Smith**.
5. **This is big business**.
6. **Bill is still ill**.
7. **This winter** was **bitter**.
8. **Give** the **list** to **Lynn**.
9. My **little sister is timid**.
10. The **picture is** a **big hit**.

SELF-TEST I   (Correct answers may be found in Appendix II on p. 291.)

Listen carefully to your teacher or the instructor on the tape as the following pairs of words are presented. **ONE** word in each pair is pronounced with [ɪ]. Circle the number of the word with the vowel [ɪ].

EXAMPLE: The instructor says: ***mitt   meat***
You circle: ①   2

1. 1   2
2. 1   2
3. 1   2
4. 1   2
5. 1   2

REVIEW OF [i] AND [ɪ]

ORAL EXERCISE

Repeat the pairs of words and sentences carefully after your teacher or the instructor on the tape. REMEMBER to SMILE and feel the tension in your lips when you repeat the words with [i] and to RELAX your muscles as you pronounce the [ɪ] words.

[i]	[ɪ]
1. least	list
2. seat	sit
3. heat	hit
4. feet	fit
5. leave	live

6. Heat it now.	Hit it now.
7. Change the wheel.	Change the will.
8. Did you feel it?	Did you fill it?
9. The meal was big.	The mill was big.
10. He will leave.	He will live.

11. Please **sit** in the **seat**.
        [ɪ]   [i]
12. He **did** a good **deed**.
        [ɪ]   [i]
13. **Phil** doesn't **feel** well.
        [ɪ]   [i]
14. **Lynn** ate **lean** meat.
        [ɪ]   [i]
15. Potato **chips** are **cheap**.
            [ɪ]   [i]

SELF-TEST I (Correct answers may be found in Appendix II on p. 291.)

Your teacher or the instructor on the tape will say only **ONE** word in each of the following pairs. Listen carefully and circle the word that you hear.

EXAMPLE A: (meat) mit
EXAMPLE B: feel (fill)

1. field   filled
2. bean   bin
3. neat   knit
4. deal   dill
5. beat   bit

SELF-TEST II (Correct answers may be found in Appendix II on p. 291.)

Your teacher or the instructor on the tape will present the following sentences using ONLY ONE of the choices. Listen carefully and circle the word (and vowel) used.

EXAMPLE: You need a new   (wheel   (will).
                                   [i]   [ɪ]

1. They cleaned the   (sheep   ship).
                             [i]   [ɪ]

2. Will he   (leave   live)?
                             [i]   [ɪ]

3. The boy was   (beaten   bitten).
                             [i]   [ɪ]

4. His clothes are   (neat   knit).
                             [i]   [ɪ]

5. She has plump   (cheeks   chicks).
                             [i]   [ɪ]

SELF-TEST III   (Correct answers may be found in Appendix II on p. 292.)

Read each of the following sentences aloud. In the brackets above each boldface word, write the phonetic symbol ([i] or [ɪ]) representing the vowel in that word. **This self-test is not on the tape.**

           [i]   [ɪ]   [ɪ]

EXAMPLE: The **field** was **filled with** flowers.

       [ ] [ ]   [ ]
1. Take a **dip in** the **deep** water.
       [ ]   [ ]   [ ]
2. They **picked Tim** for the **team**.
      [ ]   [ ]   [ ]   [ ]
3. **Please beat** the **sweet cream**.
     [ ] [ ] [ ][ ]   [ ]
4. **She will sit in** the **seat**.
       [ ]   [ ]   [ ]
5. The **heat** wave **hit** the **city**.

FOR AN ENCORE . . . .

CONVERSATION

Plan at least three occasions when you have to use phrases of introduction. Use the following key phrases:

"This is (my sister Jill) _____" (name of person).
"Pleased to meet you, (Mr./Mrs./Miss Smith) _____" (name).
"I'd like you to meet (my friend Tim, my sister, etc.) _____."

You can also use the phrase *"This is _____"* when identifying yourself on the phone. (*"This is Kim."*)

REMEMBER TO KEEP PRACTICING!!!

      ⟨⟨WE GUARANTEE IT'S EASY TO SAY [ɪ] AND [i]⟩⟩

[eɪ] as in *ATE, GAME,* and *THEY*
(DICTIONARY MARK: ā)

PRONOUNCING [eɪ]

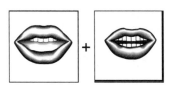

LIPS:	are spread, not rounded.
JAW:	rises with the tongue and closes slightly.
TONGUE:	glides from midlevel to near the roof of the mouth.

[eɪ] is a dipthong. It begins with [e] and ends with [ɪ].

POSSIBLE PRONUNCIATION PROBLEMS

Pronunciation problems occur because of confusing English spelling patterns and the similarity of [eɪ] and [ɛ] (the sound to be described in the next chapter).

EXAMPLE: When you substitute [ɛ] for [eɪ]   **late**   becomes **let**.
paper becomes **pepper**.

With practice, you will s<u>ay</u> [eɪ] the right w<u>ay</u>.

EXERCISE A

The following words should all be pronounced with [eɪ]. Repeat them carefully after your teacher or the instructor on the tape.

[eɪ] At the Beginning	**[eɪ] In the Middle**	**[eɪ] At the End**
ate	same	way
ape	rain	say
age	came	day
aim	lake	May
eight	date	obey

[eɪ] Spelled:

"a"	**"ai"**	**"ay"**	**"eigh"**
late	main	day	eight
sane	fail	bay	weigh
safe	wait	hay	sleigh
hate	grain	ray	freight
lady	raise	play	neighbor

Less frequent spelling patterns for [eɪ] consist of the letters *ea*, *ey*, and *ei*.

EXAMPLES: br**ea**k gr**ea**t th**ey** gr**ey** v**ei**n

> **HINTS:**
> a. When *a* is in a syllable ending in silent *e*, the letter *a* is pronounced [eɪ] (the same as the alphabet letter A!!!).
>
> EXAMPLES: s**a**me n**a**me c**a**se l**a**ne b**a**ke
>
> b. The letters *ay*, *ai*, and *ey* are usually pronounced [eɪ].
>
> EXAMPLES: pl**ay** aw**ay** b**ai**t **ai**m th**ey**
>
> c. The letters *ei* followed by *g* or *n* are usually pronounced [eɪ].
>
> EXAMPLES: w**ei**gh n**ei**ghbor v**ei**n r**ei**ndeer

The boldface words in the following phrases and sentences should all be pronounced with the diphthong [eɪ]. Repeat them carefully after your teacher or the instructor on the tape.

1. **Wake** up!
2. **gain weight**
3. What's your **name**?
4. **late date**
5. **Take** it **away**!
6. **Make haste** not **waste**!
7. **April** showers bring **May** flowers.
8. **They played** a **great game**.
9. **Blake** got an "A" on his **paper**.
10. The **lady's age** is **eighty-eight**.

SELF-TEST I   (Correct answers may be found in Appendix II on p. 292.)

Read the following *"shopping list"* out loud. (You are going to buy the items with the [eɪ] sound.) Circle **ONLY** the items pronounced with [eɪ]. **This self-test is not on the tape.**

(steak)	lettuce	mayonnaise	cereal
bread	raisins	melon	bananas
cake	tomatoes	bacon	baking soda
potatoes	crackers	peas	ice cream
grapes	celery	gravy	carrots
toothpaste	peas	squash	paper plates

SELF-TEST II

(Correct answers may be found in Appendix II on p. 292.)

Read each four-word series out loud. Circle the **ONE** word in each group of four that is **NOT** pronounced with [eɪ]. **This self-test is not on the tape.**

EXAMPLE: April   May   vacation   (sad)

1. practice   plate   play   place
2. stay   aid   plaid   raid
3. neighbor   freight   height   eighty
4. head   great   break   came
5. shave   any   staple   pays
6. America   Asia   Spain   Maine
7. laid   crayon   seven   tame
8. great   grace   grey   greedy
9. obtain   awake   create   breakfast
10. snake   obey   breath   complain

SELF-TEST III

(Correct answers may be found in Appendix II on p. 292.)

Listen carefully to your teacher or the instructor on the tape as the following paragraph is read. Circle all words pronounced with [eɪ].

· ·

(Babe) Ruth was a (famous) baseball player. He was born and raised in an orphanage in Baltimore. He first played for the Boston Red Sox but was later traded to the New York Yankees. He made 714 home runs and became a baseball legend. He was named to the Baseball Hall of Fame. The last team he played for was the Boston Braves. He died in 1948. Many say he was the greatest player of his day.

· ·

After checking your answers in Appendix II, read the paragraph aloud. Concentrate on the correct pronunciation of the [eɪ] words.

FOR AN ENCORE . . . .

READING

Turn to the sports section of your newspaper. Read about any game that was recently played. Underline all words pronounced with [eɪ]. Tape yourself reading the article aloud or read it to a friend. Practice the [eɪ] words several times.

PRACTICE MAKES PERFECT!!!
《SAY [eɪ] THE RIGHT WAY.》

[ɛ] as in *EGG, PET,* and *HEAD*
DICTIONARY MARK: ē or e

PRONOUNCING [ɛ]

LIPS: are slightly spread, not rounded.

JAW: is open more than for [eɪ].

TONGUE: is midlevel in the mouth.

POSSIBLE PRONUNCIATION PROBLEMS

Pronunciation problems occur because of confusing English spelling patterns and the similarity between [ɛ] and other sounds.

EXAMPLE A: If you replace [ɛ] with [eɪ]:   **pen** sounds like **pain**.
EXAMPLE B: If you replace [ɛ] with [æ]:   **met** sounds like **mat**.

When pronouncing [ɛ], open your mouth **wider** than for [eɪ] but less than for [æ] (the sound to be discussed in the next chapter). **Practice and you'll never make an error on** [ɛ].

EXERCISE A

The following words should all be pronounced with [ɛ]. Repeat them carefully after your teacher or the instructor on the tape.*

[ɛ] At the Beginning	[ɛ] In the Middle
any	bed
end	next
egg	west
edge	bent
else	many

*The vowel [ɛ] does not occur at the end of words in English.

[ε] Spelled:

"e"	"ea"
yes	head
red	lead
sell	dead
seven	meadow
never	measure

Less frequent spelling patterns for [ε] consist of the letters *a*, *ai*, *ie*, *ue*, and *eo*.

EXAMPLES: <u>a</u>ny ag<u>ai</u>n fr<u>ie</u>nd g<u>ue</u>st l<u>eo</u>pard

> ***HINTS:*** a. The most common spelling pattern for [ε] is the letter *e*
> before a consonant in a stressed syllable.
>
>   EXAMPLES: l<u>e</u>t am<u>e</u>nd att<u>e</u>ntive pl<u>e</u>nty
>
> b. The letter *e* before "l" is usually pronounced [ε].
>
>   EXAMPLES: w<u>e</u>ll t<u>e</u>lephone f<u>e</u>lt s<u>e</u>ldom
>
> c. The letters *ea* before *d* are usually pronounced [ε].
>
>   EXAMPLES: thr<u>ea</u>d ah<u>ea</u>d r<u>ea</u>dy d<u>ea</u>d

 EXERCISE B

Repeat the following pairs of words after your teacher or the instructor on the tape. When pronouncing the words with [ε], be sure to lower your jaw a bit more than for [eɪ].

[ε]	[eɪ]
met	mate
bet	bait
fed	fade
pen	pain
wet	weight

EXERCISE C

The boldface words in the following phrases and sentences should all be pronounced with the vowel [ɛ]. Repeat them carefully after your teacher or the instructor on the tape.

1. You **said** it!
2. **head** of **lettuce**
3. **best friend**
4. **healthy** and **wealthy**
5. **bent fender**
6. **never better**
7. **Breakfast** is **ready** at **ten**.
8. **Ted left** a **message**.
9. **Let** me **get** some **rest**!
10. Don't **forget** to **send** the **letter**.

SELF-TEST I   (Correct answers may be found in Appendix II on p. 293.)

Listen carefully as your teacher or the instructor on the tape presents five sentences. Some words that should be pronounced with [ɛ] will be said INCORRECTLY. Circle **C** for "**Correct**" or **I** for "**Incorrect**" to indicate whether the [ɛ] word in each sentence is pronounced properly.

Sentence #	Response		
EXAMPLE A:	Ⓒ	I	(Who **fed** the fish?)
EXAMPLE B:	C	Ⓘ	(I got **wait** in the rain.)
1.	C	I	
2.	C	I	
3.	C	I	
4.	C	I	
5.	C	I	

SELF-TEST II

(Correct answers may be found in Appendix II on p. 293.)

Read the following dialogue aloud. Circle all words that should be pronounced with the vowel [ɛ]. **This self-test is not on the tape.**

....

MS. NELSON: "(Nelson) (Temporary) (Help.") Ms. Nelson speaking. Can I help you?

MR. EVANS: Yes, this is Mr. Evans. I need a temporary secretary.

MS. NELSON: What kind of secretary do you need?

MR. EVANS: The BEST! That means well educated and with excellent clerical skills.

MS. NELSON: Anything else?

MR. EVANS: Yes. I like pretty secretaries with good legs. Get what I mean?

MS. NELSON: Yes, I do. I have the best secretary for you. I'll send one Wednesday at ten.

MR. EVANS: Thanks. It's been a pleasure talking to you.

MS. NELSON: Evelyn, get me Ted Benson's file. He's an excellent secretary and has very good legs!!!

....

After checking your answers in Appendix II, practice the dialogue out loud again. This time, try it with a friend! Carefully pronounce all [ɛ] words.

FOR AN ENCORE . . . .

LISTENING

Listen to the weather report on radio or TV. Make a list of all the words you hear pronounced with [ɛ]. After the broadcast, practice them aloud (for example, t*e*mperature, w*ea*ther, w*e*t, s*e*venty degrees, etc.).

PRACTICE YOUR [ɛ] AGAIN AND AGAIN AND . . .

《YOU'LL N*E*VER MAKE AN *E*RROR ON [ɛ].》

[æ] as in *AT, FAT,* and *HAPPY*
(DICTIONARY MARK: a or ă)

PRONOUNCING [æ]

LIPS: are spread.

JAW: is open more than for [ɛ].

TONGUE: is low near the floor the mouth.

POSSIBLE PRONUNCIATION PROBLEMS

The vowel [æ] might not exist in your language and may be difficult for you to hear and produce. Also, irregular English spelling patterns are likely to cause confusion.

EXAMPLES: If you say [a] instead of [æ]: **hat** will sound like **hot.**
If you say [ɛ] instead of [æ]: **bad** will sound like **bed.**

When producing the vowel [æ], remember to spread your lips and open your mouth. But—don't open it too wide or you will find yourself substituting [a] (the vowel to be studied in the next chapter) instead! *PRACTICE, PRACTICE, PRACTICE AND you'll HAVE [æ] down PAT!!!*

EXERCISE A

The following words should all be pronounced with the [æ] sound. Repeat them as accurately as possible after your teacher or the instructor on the tape.*

[æ] At the Beginning	[æ] In the Middle
at	cat
am	map
and	have
ask	back
after	happy

A less frequent spelling pattern for [æ] consists of the letters *au*.

EXAMPLES: la<u>u</u>gh   la<u>u</u>ghter

 EXERCISE B

Repeat the following pairs of words after your teacher or the instructor on the tape. When repeating the [æ] words, be sure to open your mouth more than for [ɛ].

[æ]	[ɛ]
had	head
mat	met
pat	pet
past	pest
tan	ten

*The vowel [æ] does not occur at the end of words in English.

 **EXERCISE C**

The boldface words in the following phrases and sentences should all be pronounced with the vowel [æ]. Repeat them carefully after your teacher or the instructor on the tape.

1. **last chance**
2. I'll be **back**.
3. **at** a **glance**
4. **Wrap** it up.
5. Is **that** a **fact**?
6. **Clap** your **hands**.
7. **Hand** me a **pack** of **matches**.
8. I **have** to **catch** a **cab**.
9. **Sam can't stand** the **man**.
10. The **gambler** plays **black jack**.

 **SELF-TEST I**   (Correct answers may be found in Appendix II on p. 293.)

Listen carefully to your teacher or the instructor on the tape as each three-word series is presented. Only ONE word in each series will have the [æ] vowel. Circle the number of the word with the [æ] sound.

EXAMPLE: Your teacher says: *knack*   *knock*   *neck*

             You circle: ①   2   3

1. 1 2 3
2. 1 2 3
3. 1 2 3
4. 1 2 3
5. 1 2 3

Read the following letter aloud. Circle all words that should be pronounced with the vowel [æ]. **This self-test is not on the tape.**

··

Dear Mom (and) (Dad.)

At last we are in San Francisco. It's a fabulous city! As we stand at the top of Telegraph Hill we can see Alcatraz. We plan to catch a cable car and visit Grant Avenue in Chinatown. After that, we'll have tea in the Japanese Gardens. Yesterday we drank wine in Napa Valley. We also passed through the National Park. Our last stop is Disneyland in Los Angeles. We'll be back next Saturday.

Love,

Gladys

P.S. We need cash. Please send money fast!

··

After checking your answers in Appendix II, practice reading the letter again. Concentrate on the correct pronunciation of the [æ] words.

FOR AN ENCORE ·

READING

Select a set of directions for something (for using an appliance, assembling an item, etc.). Circle all words pronounced with [æ]. Read the directions aloud step by step to another person. Ask the person to repeat the directions back to you. Practice the words your listener has difficulty understanding.

PR<u>A</u>CTICE, PR<u>A</u>CTICE, PR<u>A</u>CTICE <u>A</u>ND . . .

⟨⟨YOU'LL H<u>A</u>VE [æ] DOWN P<u>A</u>T!⟩⟩

[a] as in *ARM*, *HOT*, and *FATHER*
(DICTIONARY MARK: ä or ŏ)

PRONOUNCING [a]

LIPS: are completely apart in a "*yawning*" position.

JAW: is lower than for any other vowel.

TONGUE: is flat on the floor of the mouth.

POSSIBLE PRONUNCIATION PROBLEMS

Irregular English spelling patterns are the main reason you have pronunciation problems with the vowel [a]. The letter *o* in English is frequently pronounced [a].

EXAMPLE A: If you substitute [ou] for [a]: **not** will sound like **note**.
EXAMPLE B: If you substitute [ʌ] for [a]: **not** will sound like **nut**.
EXAMPLE C: If you substitute [ɔ] for [a]: **cot** will sound like **caught**.

Remember to open your mouth **wider** than for any other vowel. *We're* **P_OSITIVE you'll be _ON T_ARGET with [a]** !

EXERCISE A

The following words should all be pronounced with [a]. Repeat them accurately after your teacher or the instructor on the tape.*

[a] At the Beginning	[a] In the Middle
on	top
odd	cot
arm	shop
oxen	wasp
honest	watch

*The vowel [a] does not occur at the end of words in English.

[a] Spelled:

"a"	"o"
want	fox
wallet	hot
dark	spot
farther	opera
pardon	follow

> **HINTS:**   a. The letter *o* followed by *b*, *d*, *g*, *p*, *t*, or *ck* is usually pronounced [a].
>
>   EXAMPLES: ro<u>b</u>in   ro<u>d</u>   lo<u>g</u>   sto<u>p</u>   lo<u>t</u>   po<u>ck</u>et
>
>   b. The letter *a* followed by *r* is usually pronounced [a].
>
>   EXAMPLES: f<u>ar</u>m   al<u>ar</u>m   c<u>ar</u>t   st<u>ar</u>t   <u>are</u>

EXERCISE B

Repeat the following pairs of words after your teacher or the instructor on the tape. Be sure to open your mouth **wider** when pronouncing the words with the [a] vowel.

[a]	[æ]
cop	cap
hot	hat
pot	pat
odd	add
mop	map

 **EXERCISE C**

The boldface words in the following phrases and sentences should all be pronounced with the vowel [a]. Repeat them as accurately as possible after your teacher or the instructor on the tape.

1. **hot pot**
2. **stock market**
3. **not far apart**
4. **top** to **bottom**
5. **cops** and **robbers**
6. **Park** the **car**.
7. It was **hard** to **start** the **car**.
8. The **doctor wants** to **operate**.
9. **Tom wants** to **shop**.
10. My **watch stopped**.

 **SELF-TEST I**   (Correct answers may be found in Appendix II on p. 294.)

You are a photographer for a well known magazine! Your assignment is to photograph animals whose names contain the vowel [a]. Repeat the names of the following "creatures" after your teacher or the instructor on the tape. Circle only animals pronounced with [a].

(condor)	(collie)	leopard	llama
cat	tiger	hippopotamus	dolphin
fox	iguana	lobster	octopus

SELF-TEST II

(Correct answers may be found in Appendix II on p. 294.)

Read the following dialogue aloud. Circle all words that should be pronounced with the [a] vowel. **This self-test is not on the tape.**

....

DONNA: (Bob,) I (want) to talk to you.

BOB: Are you all right?

DONNA: Don't be alarmed. I saw Dr. Johnson at the hospital. You're going to be a father!!!! Our new baby will be born on October 5th.

BOB: I'm in shock. How do you feel?

DONNA: I'm feeling "on top of the world." I've got a list of names for our new baby.

BOB: If it's a girl, let's call her Donna after her Mom.

DONNA: "Donna" is fine for a middle name. How about Connie or Barbara as her first name?

BOB: To be honest, I'm fond of the name Barbara. But you forgot that we might have a boy. How about Bob Junior?

DONNA: I like the name Bob a lot! How about Tom or John for his middle name?

BOB: OK, our girl will be Barbara Donna Scott. We can call her "Bobbie" for short.

DONNA: If it's a boy, his name will be Robert John Scott and we can still use the nickname "Bobby."

BOB: Stop—what if we have twins?

DONNA: I'm NOT ready for that problem. Watching one little tot will be enough, Pop!

....

FOR AN ENCORE . . . .

LISTENING

Listen to your favorite newscaster on radio or TV. Specifically listen for all the words pronounced with [a]. List as many as you can in a period of three minutes. Practice your list of [a] words aloud.

COMPLETE ALL THE ACTIVITIES AND . . .

⟨⟨WE'RE POSITIVE YOU'LL BE ON TARGET WITH [a]!⟩⟩

REVIEW OF [eɪ] [ɛ] [æ] AND [a]

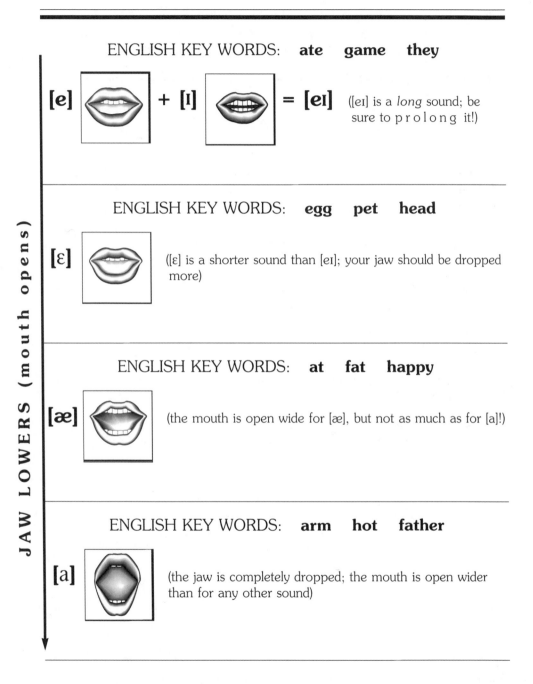

ENGLISH KEY WORDS: **ate**   **game**   **they**

[e] + **[ɪ]** = **[eɪ]**   ([eɪ] is a *long* sound; be sure to p r o l o n g it!)

ENGLISH KEY WORDS: **egg**   **pet**   **head**

[ɛ]   ([ɛ] is a shorter sound than [eɪ]; your jaw should be dropped more)

ENGLISH KEY WORDS: **at**   **fat**   **happy**

[æ]   (the mouth is open wide for [æ], but not as much as for [a]!)

ENGLISH KEY WORDS: **arm**   **hot**   **father**

[a]   (the jaw is completely dropped; the mouth is open wider than for any other sound)

JAW LOWERS (mouth opens)

REVIEW EXERCISE

Repeat the rows of words and sentences accurately after your teacher or the instructor on the tape. Feel your mouth open wider as you progress through the pronunciation of the [eɪ], [ɛ], [æ], and [a] words.

MOUTH OPENS WIDER ⟶

[eɪ]	[ɛ]	[æ]	[a]
1. *a*id	*E*d	*a*dd	*o*dd
2. r*a*ke	wr*e*ck	r*a*ck	r*o*ck
3. p*ai*d	p*e*d	p*a*d	p*o*d
4. N*a*te	n*e*t	gn*a*t*	n*o*t
5. p*ai*ned	p*e*nned	p*a*nned	p*o*nd

6. I h**a**te wearing a h**a**t when it's h**o**t.
    [eɪ]   [æ]   [a]

7. The house at the l**a**ke l**a**cks a l**o**ck.
             [eɪ] [æ]   [a]

8. R**o**n r**a**n in the r**ai**n.
   [a] [æ]   [eɪ]

9. It's **o**dd that **E**d can't **a**dd.
    [a]   [ɛ]   [æ]

10. D**a**n, the gr**ea**t D**a**ne, sleeps in the d**e**n.
    [æ]   [eɪ] [eɪ]   [ɛ]

*A flying insect smaller than a mosquito that can bite or sting.

REVIEW TEST I   (Correct answers may be found in Appendix II on p. 294.)

Your teacher or the instructor on the tape will present the following sentences using ONE of the words in parentheses. Listen carefully and circle the word (and vowel) used.

EXAMPLE: I'll write that   (letter   (later)).
                             [ɛ]   [eɪ]

1. Leave the car in the   (shed shade).
                             [ɛ]   [eɪ]

2. Do you know what was (sad said)?
                             [æ]   [ɛ]

3. We need more   (paper pepper).
                             [eɪ]   [ɛ]

4. Please clear that   (debt date).
                             [ɛ]   [eɪ]

5. Children like   (pets pats).
                             [ɛ]   [æ]

Now that you have completed the review test, read each of the sentences twice. Carefully pronounce the first word in parentheses in the first reading and the contrast word in the second reading.

REVIEW TEST II   (Correct answers may be found in Appendix II on p. 295.)

Read the following words aloud. Write each word under the symbol that represents the vowel sound of the boldface letter(s). **This review test is not on the tape**.

m**a**tch	fr**ei**ght	w**a**tch	bl**o**nde	**A**pril
sh**o**ck	p**a**rt	v**a**st	f**o**x	**a**pple
pl**a**ne	h**a**lf	**e**gg	c**a**n't	t**o**p
b**e**ll	st**ea**k	l**au**gh	pl**ai**d	st**a**ple
g**ue**ss	**a**ny	v**ei**l	s**ai**d	h**e**lp
w**a**sp	n**a**me	fr**ie**nd	**ai**d	st**o**p

[eɪ] as in *ATE*   [ɛ] as in *EGG*   [æ] as in *HAT*   [a] as in *HOT*

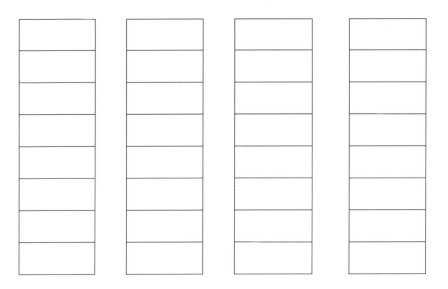

After checking your answers in Appendix II, carefully pronounce all of the words again.

[u] as in *YOU, TOO,* and *RULE*
(DICTIONARY MARK: o͞o)
and
[ʊ] as in *COOK* and *PUT*
(DICTIONARY MARK: oo or o͝o)

PRONOUNCING [u]

LIPS: are tense and in a "whistling" position.

JAW: is completely raised.

TONGUE: is high near the roof of the mouth.

POSSIBLE PRONUNCIATION PROBLEMS

Pronunciation problems occur because of confusing English spelling patterns and the similarity of [u] and [ʊ] (the sound to be described next).

EXAMPLES: When you substitute [ʊ] for [u]: **pool** becomes **pull**.

  suit becomes **soot**.

YOU CAN DO IT! Your lips should be tense and in a "whistling" position. **[u] *is a LONG sound; be sure to p r o l o n g it. If you remember to PROTRUDE your lips when PRODUCING [u], YOU'LL never CONFUSE "pull" with "POOL"!***

EXERCISE A

The following words should all be pronounced with [u]. Repeat them carefully after your teacher or the instructor on the tape.

[u] In the Middle	[u] At the End
food	do
pool	new
room	you
suit	shoe
goose	chew

[u] spelled:

"u"	"oo"	"o"	"ew"	"ue"
rule	cool	do	new	due
rude	fool	to	drew	blue
June	too	who	stew	clue
tune	noon	tomb	knew	glued
tuna	stool	lose	news	avenue

> **NOTE:** When the letter *u* follows *t, d, n,* or *s,* some Americans pronounce it [ju].
>
> EXAMPLES: Tuesday duty suit

Less frequent spelling patterns for [u] consist of the letters *ui, ou, oe, ieu,* and *ough*.

EXAMPLES: fruit group shoe lieutenant through

> **HINTS:** a. The letters *ew* are usually pronounced [u].
>
> EXAMPLES: new stew drew grew
>
> b. The letters *oo* followed by *l, m,* or *n* are usually pronounced [u].
>
> EXAMPLES: school boom moon

> **NOTE:** When speaking English, international students frequently forget to prolong the [u] vowel before consonants.

EXERCISE B

Read the following pairs of [u] words aloud. *PROLONG* the vowel [u] before the consonant. (The dots are there to remind you to p r o l o n g the [u]. **This exercise is not on the tape.**

1. new   new...........s   (news)
2. due   due...........s   (dues)
3. sue   sue ....d   (sued)
4. who   who...........m   (whom)
5. glue   glue ....d   (glued)

 ## EXERCISE C

The boldface words in the following phrases and sentences should all be pronounced with the vowel [u]. Repeat them carefully after your teacher or the instructor on the tape.

1. What's **new**?
2. **Who** is it?
3. How are **you**?
4. **loose tooth**
5. in the **mood**
6. **School** will **soon** be **through.**
7. **You** must **chew** your **food.**
8. He **proved** he **knew** the **truth.**
9. The **group flew to New** York.
10. **Who ruined** my **new shoes**?

SELF-TEST I   (Correct answers may be found in Appendix II on p.295.)

Listen carefully to your teacher or the instructor on the tape as ten three-word series are presented. ONE word in each group will be pronounced with [u]. Circle the number of the word with the vowel [u].

EXAMPLE: The instructor says: **comb**   **cool**   **call**
You circle: 1   ②   3

1. 1 2 3
2. 1 2 3
3. 1 2 3
4. 1 2 3
5. 1 2 3
6. 1 2 3
7. 1 2 3
8. 1 2 3
9. 1 2 3
10. 1 2 3

PRONOUNCING [ʊ]

LIPS: are relaxed and slightly parted.
JAW: is slightly lower than for [u].
TONGUE: is high, but lower than for [u].

POSSIBLE PRONUNCIATION PROBLEMS

The vowel [ʊ] may be difficult for you to hear and produce. You probably substitute the more familiar [u] sound.

EXAMPLES: When you substitute [u] for [ʊ]:   **full**   sounds like **fool**.
cook sounds like **kook**.

As you repeat the exercise words, remember NOT to protrude your lips and tense them as you would for [u]. **[ʊ] *is a SHORT, QUICK sound; your lips should barely move while saying it. Practice [ʊ] as you SH<u>OU</u>LD, and you'll be UNDERST<u>OO</u>D!!!***

EXERCISE A

The following words should all be pronounced with [ʊ]. Repeat them carefully after your teacher or the instructor on the tape.* *RELAX* your lips and jaw as you produce [ʊ].

[ʊ] In the Middle

cook	put
full	wood
book	took
good	foot
stood	hood
shook	woman
push	cushion

*The vowel [ʊ] is found only in the middle of words.

[ʊ] Spelled:

"u"	"oo"	"ou"
pull	wool	could
put	wood	would
push	hook	should
bullet	good	
pudding	cookie	

A less frequent spelling pattern for [ʊ] is the letter *o*.

EXAMPLES: w<u>o</u>lf   w<u>o</u>man

HINTS: a. The letters *oo* followed by *d* or *k* are usually pronounced [ʊ].

  EXAMPLES: h<u>oo</u>d g<u>oo</u>d w<u>oo</u>d b<u>oo</u>k l<u>oo</u>k c<u>oo</u>k

  b. The letter *u* followed by *sh* is usually pronounced [ʊ].

  EXAMPLES: b<u>u</u>sh p<u>u</u>sh c<u>u</u>shion

EXERCISE B

The boldface words in the following phrases and sentences should all be pronounced with the [ʊ] vowel. Repeat them carefully after your teacher or the instructor on the tape.

1. **Look** out!
2. Take a **good look.**
3. **good-looking**
4. He **couldn't** come.
5. **Should** we go?
6. Who **took** my **book**?
7. **Put** the **wood** away.
8. He **took** a **look** at the **crook.**
9. The **woman stood** on one **foot.**
10. **Could** you eat ten **sugar cookies**?

SELF-TEST I   (Correct answers may be found in Appendix II on p. 296.)

Listen carefully as your teacher or the instructor on the tape presents ten sentences. Some words that should be pronounced with [ʊ] will be said INCORRECTLY. Circle **C** for "**CORRECT**" or **I** for "**INCORRECT**" to indicate whether the [ʊ] word in each sentence is pronounced properly.

Sentence #	Response		
EXAMPLE A:	C	(I)	(I was *fool* after eating.)
EXAMPLE B:	(C)	I	(The *cushion* is soft.)
1.	C	I	
2.	C	I	
3.	C	I	
4.	C	I	
5.	C	I	
6.	C	I	
7.	C	I	
8.	C	I	
9.	C	I	
10.	C	I	

REVIEW OF [u] and [ʊ]

ORAL EXERCISE

Repeat the pairs of words and sentences carefully after your teacher or the instructor on the tape. REMEMBER to feel tension and *PROTRUDE* your lips when you repeat the words with [u] and to *RELAX* your muscles as you pronounce the [ʊ] words.

[u]	[ʊ]
1. fool	full
2. suit	soot
3. Luke	look
4. pool	pull
5. stewed	stood

6. I hate the black **suit.**   I hate the black **soot.**
7. She went to **Luke**.   She went to **look**.
8. I have no **pool**.   I have no **pull**.
9. He's quite a **kook**!   He's quite a **cook**!
10. The beef **stewed** for an hour.   The beef **stood** for an hour.

11. Take a **good look** at **Luke**.
     [ʊ] [ʊ]   [u]

12. **Pull** him from the **pool**.
  [ʊ]   [u]

13. He has **soot** on his **suit**.
      [ʊ]   [u]

14. The **fool** was **full** of fun.
    [u]   [ʊ]

15. The horse **should** be **shoed**.
       [ʊ]   [u]

Listen carefully to your teacher or the instructor on the tape as ten three-word series are presented. Two of the words in each group will be the SAME; one will be DIFFERENT. Circle the number of the word that is **different**.

EXAMPLE: The instructor says: *should*   *should*   *shoed*

You circle: 1   2   ③

```
 1. 1  2  3
 2. 1  2  3
 3. 1  2  3
 4. 1  2  3
 5. 1  2  3
 6. 1  2  3
 7. 1  2  3
 8. 1  2  3
 9. 1  2  3
10. 1  2  3
```

SELF-TEST II   (Correct answers may be found in Appendix II on p.296.)

Read the following paragraph about *Harry Houdini* aloud. **CIRCLE** all words pronounced with [u] and **UNDERLINE** all words pronounced with [ʊ]. **This self-test is not on the tape.**

• •

Harry (Houdini) was a magician known (throughout) the world. He could remove himself from chains and ropes and could walk through walls! Houdini was born in Budapest, Hungary. He moved to New York when he was twelve and soon took up magic. Rumors spread that Houdini had supernatural powers. However, he was truthful and stated that his tricks could be understood by all humans! Houdini is an idol for all would-be magicians.

• •

After checking your answers in Appendix II, practice reading the paragraph aloud. ***REMEMBER—your lips must be in a TENSE "whistling" position for*** [u] ***and RELAXED when pronouncing*** [ʊ].

FOR AN ENCORE . . . .

READING

Read one or two headline news stories on the front page of the newspaper. Circle all [ʊ] and [u] words. Read the sentences containing the circled words aloud. Carefully pronounce the [ʊ] and [u] vowel sounds.

PRACTICE [ʊ] AND [u] AS Y_OU_ SH_OU_LD AND . . .

《Y_OU_ WILL BE UNDERST_OO_D!》

[ʌ] as in *UP, BUT,* and *COME*
(DICTIONARY MARK: u or ŭ)

PRONOUNCING [ʌ]

LIPS: are relaxed and slightly parted.

JAW: is relaxed and slightly lowered.

TONGUE: is relaxed and midlevel in the mouth.

POSSIBLE PRONUNCIATION PROBLEMS

The vowel [ʌ] may not exist in your language and may be difficult for you to hear and pronounce. It is easy to become confused by irregular English spelling patterns and to substitute sounds that are more familiar to you.

EXAMPLE A: If you say [a] instead of [ʌ]: **color** will sound like **collar**.
EXAMPLE B: If you say [oʊ] instead of [ʌ]: **come** will sound like **comb**.
EXAMPLE C: If you say [ɔ] instead of [ʌ]: **done** will sound like **dawn**.

Remember, [ʌ] is a short, quick sound. You shouldn't feel any tension and your lips should barely move during its production. *JUST relax as you say [ʌ] and you won't RUN into TROUBLE!*

EXERCISE A

The following words should all be pronounced with the [ʌ] vowel. Repeat them accurately after your teacher or the instructor on the tape.*

[ʌ] At the Beginning	[ʌ] In the Middle
us	hug
up	won
of	nut
oven	does
other	must
under	come

*The vowel [ʌ] does not exist at the end of words in English.

[ʌ] Spelled:

"u"	"o"
but	love
cut	done
sun	some
lucky	mother
funny	Monday

Less frequent spelling patterns for [ʌ] consist of the letters *ou, oo, oe,* and *a.*

EXAMPLES: c<u>ou</u>sin   tr<u>ou</u>ble   fl<u>oo</u>d   d<u>oe</u>s   w<u>a</u>s   wh<u>a</u>t

> **NOTE:**   [ʌ] is a vowel that occurs ONLY in stressed syllables of words. It does NOT occur in unstressed syllables. Therefore the following words are pronounced with the unstressed vowel [ə]* and **not** [ʌ].
>
> | a | upon | the | soda |
> |---|---|---|---|
> | alone | alike | suppose | campus |

EXERCISE B

Repeat the following pairs of words after your teacher or the instructor on the tape. When repeating the words with [ʌ], your lips must be completely relaxed and should barely move.

[ʌ]	[a]
cut	cot
come	calm
hut	hot
nut	not
pup	pop

EXERCISE C

The boldface words in the following phrases and sentences should all be pronounced with the vowel [ʌ]. Repeat them accurately after your teacher or the instructor on the tape.

1. **Come** in.
2. **What does** it mean?
3. **bubble gum**
4. **once** a **month**
5. **Once** is **enough**.
6. **cover up**
7. My **uncle** is my **mother's brother**.
8. My **cousin** is my **uncle's son**.
9. The **gloves** are **such** an **ugly color**.
10. **Come** have **some fun** in the **sun**.

---

*Refer to page 203 for a complete description of the unstressed vowel [ə].

SELF-TEST I

(Correct answers may be found in Appendix II on p. 297.)

Read the following **"lunch menu"** aloud. Select your **"lunch"** by circling the food pronounced with the [ʌ] vowel. **This self-test is not on the tape.**

....

COCKTAILS
Sake   Wine   (Rum Punch)

APPETIZERS
Stuffed Mushrooms   Shrimp Cocktail   Egg Roll

SOUPS
Won Ton   French Onion   Clam Chowder

SALADS
Hearts of Lettuce   Caesar   Tomato and Cucumber

VEGETABLES
Buttered Corn   Baked Potato   Carrots

ENTREES
Shrimp Tempura   Prime Ribs   Roast Duck

BREADS
Italian Bread   Hot Muffins   Garlic Rolls

DESSERTS
Pumpkin Pie   Vanilla Pudding   Ice Cream

BEVERAGES
Coffee   Milk   Cup of Tea

....

After checking your answers in Appendix II, practice **each** circled menu item by saying it in the sentence *"**I had** _____ **for lunch.**"*

EXAMPLE: *I had* (a) ***rum punch*** *for* **lunch.**"

Remember to pronounce all the [ʌ] *"lunch items"* carefully!

Listen carefully as your teacher or instructor on the tape presents five sentences. Some words that should be pronounced with [ʌ] will be said INCORRECTLY. Circle **C** for **"Correct"** or **I** for **"Incorrect"** to indicate whether the [ʌ] word in each sentence is pronounced properly.

EXAMPLE A: Ⓒ   I   (I **love** to watch children play.)
EXAMPLE B: C   Ⓘ   (The heavy bricks weigh a **tone**.)

1.   C   I
2.   C   I
3.   C   I
4.   C   I
5.   C   I

FOR AN ENCORE . . . .

Listening

The theme of many popular songs today is **"LOVE."** Listen to your favorite radio station, cassette, or CD. Select a "love" song and make a list of all the [ʌ] words you hear. After the song is over, practice your list of words aloud. Be sure to say the word **love** correctly. This activity can be done alone if you prefer!

JUST RELAX AS YOU SAY [ʌ] AND . . .

《**YOU WON'T RUN INTO TROUBLE WITH [ʌ]!**》

[oʊ] as in *OH, NO,* and *BOAT*
(DICTIONARY MARK: ō)

PRONOUNCING [oʊ]

LIPS: are tense and very round.

JAW: rises with the tongue and closes slightly.

TONGUE: glides from midlevel to near the roof of the mouth.

[oʊ] is a diphthong. It begins with [o] and ends with [ʊ].

POSSIBLE PRONUNCIATION PROBLEMS

Once again your pronunciation problems with this sound occur because of confusing English spelling patterns and the similarities between other vowel sounds.

EXAMPLE A: If you substitute [ʌ] for [oʊ]: **coat** will sound like **cut**.
EXAMPLE B: If you substitute [ɔ] for [oʊ]: **bold** will sound like **bald**.
EXAMPLE C: If you substitute [a] for [oʊ]: **note** will sound like **not**.

When producing the diphthong [oʊ], round your lips into the shape of the letter o! **[oʊ]** is a **LONG** sound; be sure to prolong it. ***Listen carefully to your teacher or the tapes and your [oʊ] will be OK!***

EXERCISE A

The following words should all be pronounced with [ou]. Repeat them carefully after your teacher or the instructor on the tape.

[ou] At the Beginning	[ou] In the Middle	[ou] At the End
oat	boat	go
own	both	so
oak	coat	toe
omen	nose	sew
open	known	snow

[ou] Spelled:

"o"	"oa"	"ow"	"oe"	"ou"
no	soap	know	toe	dough
rope	goat	owe	foe	though
vote	loan	grow	goes	shoulder
home	foam	throw		
fold	load	bowl		

> **HINTS:** a. When *o* is in a syllable ending in silent *e*, the letter *o* is pronounced [ou] (the same name as the alphabet letter O!!!).
>
> EXAMPLES: ph*o*ne   n*o*te   h*o*me   r*o*pe
>
> b. The letters *oa* are usually pronounced [ou].
>
> EXAMPLES: c*oa*l   b*oa*t   r*oa*sting   t*oa*ster
>
> c. The letter *o* followed by *ld* is usually pronounced [ou].
>
> EXAMPLES: c*o*ld   *o*ld   s*o*ldier   t*o*ld

EXERCISE B

Repeat the following pairs of words after your teacher or the instructor on the tape. Be sure to **P R O L O N G** the diphthong [ou].

[oʊ]	[a]
coat	cot
note	not
road	rod
owed	odd
mope	mop

EXERCISE C

The boldface words in the following phrases and sentences should all be pronounced with the diphthong [oʊ]. Repeat them carefully after your teacher or the instructor on the tape.

1. Leave me **alone**!
2. I **suppose so**.
3. **over** and **over**
4. **Hold** the **phone**.
5. **open** and **close**
6. at a **moment's notice**
7. **Tony broke** his **toe**.
8. I **sew** my **own clothes**.
9. The **tomatoes** are **homegrown**.
10. **Don't go home so** soon.

SELF-TEST I (Correct answers may be found in Appendix II on p. 297.)

Read the following list of **"household"** items out loud. (The items pronounced with [oʊ] are broken. You need to fix them!) Circle **ONLY** the broken [oʊ] items. **This self-test is not on the tape.**

⬭toaster⬭	frying pan	bookcase	freezer
clock	telephone	faucet	radio
stove	sofa	lawn mower	table
doorknob	window	television	coat rack
can opener	mixing bowl	clothes dryer	iron

After checking your answers in Appendix II, practice each **broken [oʊ]**
item by saying it in the sentence, "The _____ is **broken**."

EXAMPLE: "The **_toaster_** is **br_o_ken**."

SELF-TEST II (Correct answers may be found in Appendix II on p. 298.)

Read the following dialogue aloud. Circle all the words pronounced with
[oʊ]. **This self-test is not on the tape.**

....

JOE: (Rose,) let's (go) on a trip. We need to be (alone.)
ROSE: OK, Joe. Where should we go?
JOE: I know! We'll go to Ohio.
ROSE: Great! We'll visit my Uncle Roland.
JOE: No, it's too cold in Ohio. We'll go to Arizona.
ROSE: Fine. We'll stay with your Aunt Mona!
JOE: No, it's too hot in Arizona. Let's go to Rome.
ROSE: Oh, good! You'll meet my Cousin Tony.
JOE: No, no, no!! We won't go to Rome. Let's go to Nome, Alaska.
        We don't know anyone there!!
ROSE: You won't believe it, but I have an old friend . . .
JOE: Hold it, Rose, we won't go anywhere! I suppose we'll just stay
        home.

....

After checking your answers in Appendix II, practice the dialogue out loud
with a friend. **P r o l o n g** all [oʊ] words!

FOR AN ENCORE . . . .

Reading

Look at a map of the United States. Find as many cities and states as you
can that are pronounced with [oʊ]. Practice saying their names aloud.

PRACTICE [oʊ] _O_VER AND _O_VER!!!

《YOUR [oʊ] WILL BE _O_K!》

[ɔ] as in *ALL, CAUGHT,* and *BOSS*
(DICTIONARY MARK: ô)

PRONOUNCING [ɔ]

LIPS: are in a tense oval shape and slightly protruded.

JAW: is open more than for [oʊ].

TONGUE: is low near the floor of the mouth.

POSSIBLE PRONUNCIATION PROBLEMS

The vowel [ɔ] is another "troublemaker." Confusing English spelling patterns frequently make you substitute more familiar vowels.

EXAMPLE A: If you substitute [a] for [ɔ]: **caller** will become **collar.**
EXAMPLE B: If you substitute [oʊ] for [ɔ]: **bought** will become **boat.**

As you listen to your teacher or the tapes, your pronunciation of [ɔ] will improve. ***Remember to protrude Y<u>OUR</u> lips and drop Y<u>OUR</u> J<u>AW</u> when you say*** [ɔ]!

EXERCISE A

The following words should all be pronounced with the [ɔ] vowel. Repeat them accurately after your teacher or the instructor on the tape.

[ɔ] At the Beginning	[ɔ] In the Middle	[ɔ] At the End
all	boss	awe
off	fall	raw
also	song	law
awful	broad	saw
often	bought	flaw

[ɔ] Spelled:

"o"	"a"	"aw"	"au"
dog	fall	jaw	auto
toss	call	lawn	fault
lost	mall	dawn	cause
long	salt	drawn	pauper
offer	stall	awful	auction

Less frequent spelling patterns for [ɔ] consist of the letters *oa* and *ou*.

EXAMPLES: br_oa_d   c_ou_gh   th_ou_ght

HINTS: a. The letter *o* followed by *ff, ng,* and *ss* is usually pronounced [ɔ].

EXAMPLES: o_ff_er   o_ff_   lo_ng_   stro_ng_   lo_ss_   to_ss_ing

b. The letters *aw* are usually pronounced [ɔ].

EXAMPLES: l_aw_n   dr_aw_   _aw_ful

c. The letter *a* followed by *ll, lk, lt,* and *ld* is usually pronounced [ɔ].

EXAMPLES: ba_ll_   ta_lk_   sa_lt_   ba_ld_

EXERCISE B

Repeat the following pairs of words after your teacher or the instructor on the tape. When repeating the [ɔ] words, be sure to protrude your lips **more** than for the other sounds.

I		II	
[ɔ]	**[ou]**	**[ɔ]**	**[a]**
saw	so	for	far
law	low	stalk	stock
tall	toll	taught	tot
bald	bold	caught	cot
bought	boat	caller	collar

EXERCISE C

The boldface words in the following phrases should all be pronounced with the vowel [ɔ]. Repeat them carefully after your teacher or the instructor on the tape.

1. **Call** it **off**.
2. **Call** it quits.
3. **call** the shots
4. **Call** it a day.
5. **walk** on air
6. **all talk**
7. **walk all** over
8. It's **all wrong**.
9. It's a **lost cause**.
10. **fought off** an **awful cough**

Listen carefully to your teacher or the tape as five pairs of sentences are presented. **ONE** sentence of each pair will contain a word pronounced with the vowel [ɔ]. Circle the number of the sentence with the [ɔ] word.

EXAMPLE: The instructor says: It's in the **hall.** It's in the **hole.**
           You circle: ①   2

1.   1   2
2.   1   2
3.   1   2
4.   1   2
5.   1   2

SELF-TEST II   (Correct answers may be found in Appendix II on p. 298.)

Read the following dialogue aloud. Circle all words that should be pronounced with the vowel [ɔ]. **This self-test is not on the tape.**

....

AUDREY: Hi, (Paula) Did you hear the (awful) news? (Maude) (called) (off) her wedding to Claude!

PAULA: Why, Audrey? I thought they were getting married in August.

AUDREY: Maude kept stalling and decided Claude was the wrong man.

PAULA: Poor Claude. He must be a lost soul.

AUDREY: Oh no. He's abroad in Austria having a ball!

PAULA: I almost forgot. What about the long tablecloth we bought them?

AUDREY: I already brought it back. The cost of the cloth will cover the cost of our lunch today.

PAULA: Audrey, you're always so thoughtful!

....

After checking your answers in Appendix II, practice reading the dialogue again. Remember to protrude your lips and drop your jaw when saying [ɔ].

FOR AN ENCORE ....

Conversation

On the different occasions when you're in a store, ask the commonly heard question, "How much does it **cost?**" Whenever you discuss the subject of spending, be sure to use the word **cost** correctly.

PROTRUDE Y<u>OU</u>R LIPS AND DROP YOUR J<u>AW</u>!!!
⟨⟨PRACTICE [ɔ] <u>O</u>FTEN!⟩⟩

REVIEW OF [ʌ] [oʊ] [ɔ] AND [a]

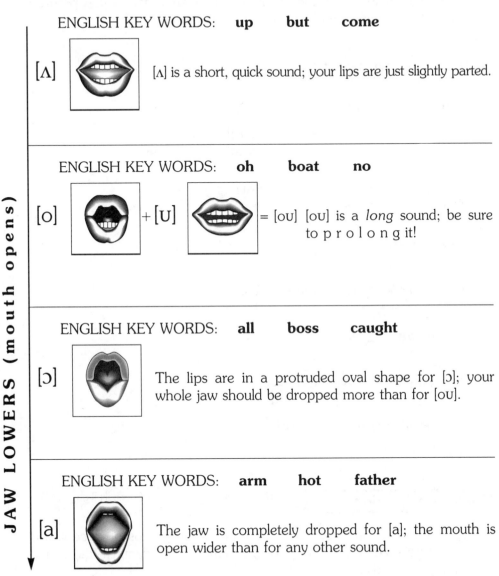

ENGLISH KEY WORDS: **up**   **but**   **come**

[ʌ]   [ʌ] is a short, quick sound; your lips are just slightly parted.

ENGLISH KEY WORDS: **oh**   **boat**   **no**

[o]   + [ʊ]   = [oʊ] [oʊ] is a *long* sound; be sure to p r o l o n g it!

ENGLISH KEY WORDS: **all**   **boss**   **caught**

[ɔ]   The lips are in a protruded oval shape for [ɔ]; your whole jaw should be dropped more than for [oʊ].

ENGLISH KEY WORDS: **arm**   **hot**   **father**

[a]   The jaw is completely dropped for [a]; the mouth is open wider than for any other sound.

JAW LOWERS (mouth opens)

Repeat the rows of words and sentences accurately after your teacher or the instructor on the tape. Feel your mouth open wider as you progress through the pronunciation of the [ʌ], [oʊ], [ɔ], and [a] words.

MOUTH OPENS WIDER ──────────────────→

[ʌ]	[oʊ]	[ɔ]	[a]
1. cut	coat	caught	cot
2. nut	note	naught	not
3. mud	mode	Maude	mod
4. fund	phoned	fawned	fond
5. Chuck	choke	chalk	chock

6. Don was done at dawn.
    [a]   [ʌ]   [ɔ]

7. Maude mowed the lawn in the mud.
    [ɔ]   [oʊ]   [ʌ]

8. Bud bought a boat.
    [ʌ]   [ɔ]   [oʊ]

9. She caught her coat on the cot.
          [ɔ]   [oʊ]   [a]

10. The caller's collar is a nice color.
      [ɔ]   [a]   [ʌ]

■□■ **REVIEW TEST I**   (Correct answers may be found in Appendix II on p. 298.)

Listen carefully to your teacher or the tape as ten groups of three words each are presented. Circle the phonetic symbol that identifies the sound each group of words has in common.

Pronunciation Key: [ʌ] as in ***BUT***   [ɔ] as in ***ALL***
                           [oʊ] as in ***NO***   [a] as in ***HOT***

Group #	Correct Phonetic Symbol						
EXAMPLE A:	[ʌ]	[oʊ]	([ɔ])	[a]	(call	story	fought)
EXAMPLE B:	[ʌ]	([oʊ])	[ɔ]	[a]	(joke	own	shows)
1.	[ʌ]	[oʊ]	[ɔ]	[a]			
2.	[ʌ]	[oʊ]	[ɔ]	[a]			
3.	[ʌ]	[oʊ]	[ɔ]	[a]			
4.	[ʌ]	[oʊ]	[ɔ]	[a]			
5.	[ʌ]	[oʊ]	[ɔ]	[a]			
6.	[ʌ]	[oʊ]	[ɔ]	[a]			
7.	[ʌ]	[oʊ]	[ɔ]	[a]			
8.	[ʌ]	[oʊ]	[ɔ]	[a]			
9.	[ʌ]	[oʊ]	[ɔ]	[a]			
10.	[ʌ]	[oʊ]	[ɔ]	[a]			

REVIEW TEST II (Correct answers may be found in Appendix II on p. 299.)

Read the following limericks aloud. In the brackets above each italicized word, write the phonetic symbol that represents the sound of the boldface letter(s). **This review test is not on the tape.**

Pronunciation Key: [ʌ] as in **UP**   [ɔ] as in **ALL**
[oʊ] as in **NO**   [a] as in **HOT**

•••

          [ʌ]   [ʌ]
A Man *From* Kent*u*cky
                    [ ]   [ ]
A man from *Kentucky* named *Bud*
     [ ]   [ ] [ ]   [ ]
Had a *lucky young son* named *Jud*
                    [ ]
When he bet on a *horse*
          [ ]   [ ]
It never *lost*, of *course*
     [ ]   [ ]   [ ]
But *one* day it got *stuck* in the *mud*!

[ ] [ ]   [ ]   [ ]
Tom's father was a *farmer* named *Bob*
      [ ]   [ ]   [ ]
Who *got* very confused *on* the *job*
    [ ]
Among his misdeeds
              [ ]
Was mixing *some* seeds
        [ ]   [ ]   [ ]
His *squash* tasted like *corn* on the *cob*!

LIMERICKS by P. W. Dale

[ə] as in *A*, *UPON*, and *SODA*
(DICTIONARY MARK: ə)

PRONOUNCING [ə]

[ə] is the sound that results when ANY vowel in English is unstressed in a word. The vowels in all unaccented syllables almost always sound like [ə]. Any letters or combination of letters can represent the schwa [ə].

The schwa vowel is a VERY short, quick sound. Your lips should be completely relaxed and barely move during its production.

POSSIBLE PRONUNCIATION PROBLEMS

In most languages, vowels are pronounced clearly and distinctly. The schwa [ə] does not exist. In English, unstressed vowels should receive much less force than other vowels in the word. In order to sound like a native English speaker, you must obscure any vowels that are **NOT** in accented syllables of words. Vowel reduction to [ə] is not sloppy speech. It is an important feature of spoken English.

EXERCISE A

Repeat the following words after your teacher or the instructor on the tape. Notice how the syllable with the [ə] vowel receives LESS stress than the other syllables in the word.

[ə] In the First Syllable	[ə] In the Middle Syllable	[ə] In the Final Syllable
a**go**	**ag**ony	**so**da
a**way**	**hol**iday	**so**fa
a**maze**	**comp**any	**ze**bra
u**pon**	**buff**alo	**fam**ous
con**tain**	**pho**tograph	**cou**sin

[ə] Spelled:

"a"	"e"	"i"	"o"	"u"
arrive	oven	liquid	occur	upon
ashamed	open	humid	obtain	suppose
asleep	cement	capital	lemon	circus
away	jacket	typical	lesson	column
signal	darkness		contain	

Other spellings of words containing [ə] include *eo, ou, iou,* and *ai.*

EXAMPLES: pig_eo_n fam_ou_s delic_iou_s nat_io_n cert_ai_n

> **NOTE:** The schwa [ə] can occur more than once and be represented by different letters in the same word.
>
> EXAMPLES: pres_i_d_e_nt el_e_ph_a_nt acc_i_d_e_nt

EXERCISE B

Read the following common phrases and sentences aloud. Be sure to pronounce the syllable with [ə] with LESS force than the other syllables. **This
exercise is not on the tape.**

1. How are you today?
2. See you tonight.
3. See you tomorrow.
4. Don't complain.
5. I suppose so.
6. I suppose it's possible.
7. Consider my complaint.
8. Complete today's lesson.
9. Don't complain about the problem.
10. My cousin will arrive at seven.

 SELF-TEST I   (Correct answers may be found in Appendix II on p. 299.)

Repeat the following words after your teacher or the instructor on the tape.
Circle the schwa vowel [ə] in the ONE unstressed syllable in each word.

EXAMPLE A: t e l ⓔ g r a p h
EXAMPLE B: r a b b ⓘ t

1. a l p h a b e t
2. u t i l i z e
3. d e p e n d i n g
4. p h o t o g r a p h
5. p a p a

SELF-TEST II   (Correct answers may be found in Appendix II on p. 299.)

Read each four-word series aloud. Circle the **ONE** word in each group of four that does **NOT** contain [ə]. **This self-test is not on the tape.**

EXAMPLE:	(slipper)	soda	finally	agree
1.	about	oven	create	olive
2.	minute	second	seven	leaving
3.	attic	attend	allow	annoy
4.	something	support	supply	suppose
5.	combine	complete	camper	compare
6.	Canada	Georgia	Tennessee	Wyoming
7.	lavender	maroon	yellow	orange
8.	strawberry	banana	vanilla	chocolate
9.	lettuce	tomato	carrot	cucumber
10.	giraffe	zebra	monkey	camel

FOR AN ENCORE . . . .

Reading

Open a book you are reading to any page. Choose any five lines on the page and circle all words pronounced with [ə]. Read the five lines aloud. Be sure to **"unstress"** the [ə] vowel in the circled words. Repeat any words you have difficulty with.

*You're really making progress. **KEEP UP THE GREAT WORK!** Why don't you take a coffee break at this point?* **YOU DESERVE IT!**

[ɝ] as in *URN, FIRST,* and *SERVE*
(DICTIONARY MARK: ûr)
and
[ɚ] as in *FATHER* and *ACTOR*
(DICTIONARY MARK: ər)

PRONOUNCING [ɝ]

LIPS:	**are protruded and slightly parted.**
JAW:	**is slightly lowered.**
TONGUE:	**is midlevel in the mouth.**

[ɝ] is a sound that occurs only in stressed syllables of words.

POSSIBLE PRONUNCIATION PROBLEMS

The vowel [ɝ] does not exist in most languages. Just remember that [ɝ] always receives strong emphasis and is found only in stressed syllables and words. It is produced with slightly protruded lips and tense tongue muscles. **Be s<u>ure</u> to practice and you'll be c<u>er</u>tain to l<u>ear</u>n [ɝ]!!!**

EXERCISE A

The following words should be pronounced with [ɝ]. Repeat them carefully after your teacher or the instructor on the tape. Your tongue tip must not touch any part of the roof of your mouth as you pronounce [ɝ].

[ɝ] At the Beginning	[ɝ] In the Middle	[ɝ] At the End
urn	turn	fur
herb	word	blur
earn	verb	stir
urgent	curve	occur
earnest	circus	prefer

[ɝ] Spelled:

"ir"	"ur"	"er"
bird	hurt	fern
girl	curl	term
firm	curb	stern
third	purple	German
circle	turkey	servant

Less frequent spelling patterns for [ɝ] consist of the letters *ear, our,* and *or.*

EXAMPLES: h<u>ear</u>d   j<u>our</u>ney   w<u>or</u>k

EXERCISE B

Repeat the following phrases and sentences after your teacher or the instructor on the tape. The boldface words should be pronounced with [ɝ].

1. **turn** it off
2. **heard** the **words**
3. slow as a **turtle**
4. **first** things **first**
5. the **worst** is yet to come
6. **Herb** left **work early** on **Thursday**.
7. The **early bird** catches the **worm**.
8. The **girl** saw the **circus first**.
9. The **servant served dessert**.
10. **Irma** had **her thirty-third birthday**.

SELF-TEST I   (Correct answers may be found in Appendix II on p. 300.)

The boldface words in the sentences on page 209 should be pronounced with [ɝ]. Read them aloud; fill in the blanks by selecting the correct word from the list below. **This self-test is not on the tape.**

purse   desserts
perfume   work
curly   turkey
church   verbs
bird   skirt

1. The **girl** wore a **purple**_____.
2. The **Germans** bake good_____.
3. At Thanksgiving we **serve**_____.
4. People **worship** in a_____.
5. I **heard** the **chirping** of the_____.
6. Another **word** for handbag is_____.
7. A **permanent** makes your hair_____.
8. I **prefer** the scent of that_____.
9. You should **learn** your nouns and_____.
10. A **person** collects unemployment when he is out of_____.

....

PRONOUNCING [ɚ]

It is difficult to hear the difference between [ɚ] and [ɜ] when these sounds are produced in isolation. However, [ɚ] is produced with much less force and occurs only in unstressed syllables of words.

POSSIBLE PRONUNCIATION PROBLEMS

[ɚ] does not exist in most languages. International students frequently substitute [a] for [ɚ], especially at the ends of words.

EXAMPLES: If you substitute [a] for [ɚ]: **sooner** becomes **"soonah."**
                            butter becomes **"buttah."**

The position of the lips and jaw is the same for [ɜ], but unlike the case with [ɜ], the tongue muscles are completely relaxed. [ɚ] never receives strong emphasis and is found only in unstressed syllables of words. The tip of the tongue must not touch your upper gum ridge during its pronunciation.

EXERCISE A

The following words should be pronounced with [ɚ]. Repeat them carefully after your teacher or the instructor on the tape.* Be sure to emphasize [ɚ] less than the other vowels in the words.

[ɚ] In the Middle	[ɚ] At the End
Sat<u>ur</u>day	bak<u>er</u>
lib<u>er</u>ty	butt<u>er</u>
p<u>er</u>haps	mirr<u>or</u>
s<u>ur</u>prise	moth<u>er</u>
aft<u>er</u>noon	soon<u>er</u>
butt<u>er</u>fly	teach<u>er</u>
flow<u>er</u>pot	deliv<u>er</u>
und<u>er</u>stood	weath<u>er</u>

[ɚ] Spelled:

"ar"	"er"	"or"	"ure"
sugar	after	color	nature
dollar	paper	actor	picture
collar	father	flavor	feature
regular	farmer	doctor	failure
grammar	silver	razor	measure

> *HINT:* The major spelling pattern for [ɚ] consists of the letters *ar*, *er*, and *or* when in the middle or at the ends of words.
>
> EXAMPLES: sug<u>ar</u>   adv<u>er</u>tise   summ<u>er</u>   col<u>or</u>ful   doct<u>or</u>

*The vowel [ɚ] does not occur at the beginning of words in English.

210   [ɝ] as in urn, [ɚ] as in father

EXERCISE B

Repeat the following phrases and sentences after your teacher or the instructor on the tape. The boldface words should be pronounced with the [ɚ] sound. (Remember, the syllables with [ɚ] are unstressed and should receive much less force than the rest of the word.)

1. **soon**er or **lat**er
2. **meas**ure the **sug**ar
3. **bett**er late than **nev**er
4. **consid**er the **off**er
5. **wat**er the **flow**ers
6. The **act**or was **bett**er than **ev**er.
7. Was the **aftern**oon **pap**er **deliv**ered?
8. The **raz**or is **sharp**er than the **sciss**ors.
9. **Summ**er is **warm**er than **wint**er.
10. The **theat**er showed a **wonder**ful **pict**ure.

SELF-TEST I   (Correct answers may be foundin Appendix II on p. 300.)

Read the following words aloud. Circle all the words that are pronounced with [ɚ]. **This self-test is not on the tape.**

(acre)	enter	curtain	dirty
supper	third	backward	Saturday
shirt	nurse	weather	percent

[ɝ] AND [ɚ] REVIEW TEST (Correct answers may be found in Appendix II on p. 300.)

Read the following paragraph about **Pearls** aloud. UNDERLINE all words pronounced with [ɝ] and CIRCLE all words with [ɚ]. **This self-test is not on the tape.**

....

PEARLS

The ***pearl*** is one of the most (treasured) gems. Pearls are formed inside the shells of oysters. The largest pearl fisheries are in Asia. Cultured pearls were developed by the Chinese in the twentieth century. They are larger than nature's pearls. A perfect pearl that is round and has a great luster is worth a lot of money. Perhaps a "diamond is a girl's best friend," but pearls will always win a woman's favor!

....

FOR AN ENCORE . . . .

Conversation

Make a list of all the occupations you can think of that are pronounced with [ɚ] (i.e., doct*or*, danc*er*, bank*er*, etc.). Begin a discussion with a friend about the many different professions and kinds of ***work*** people do. Every time you use someone's title, be sure to pronounce all [ɝ] and [ɚ] words correctly (i.e., ***"Mister Rogers** is a **wonderful teacher"*** or *"I saw my* ***lawyer yesterday").***

⟨⟨LEARN YOUR WORDS AND YOU'LL SOUND

BETTER THAN EVER!!!⟩⟩

[aʊ] as in *OUT, HOUSE,* and *COW*
(DICTIONARY MARK: ou)

PRONOUNCING [aʊ]

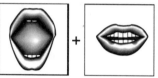

LIPS: glide from an open position.

JAW: rises with the tongue and closes.

TONGUE: glides from low to high near the roof of the mouth.

[aʊ] is a diphthong. It begins with [a] and ends with [ʊ].

POSSIBLE PRONUNCIATION PROBLEMS

[aʊ] should be easy for you to pronounce if you remember it is a diphthong which is a combination of the two vowel sounds [a] and [ʊ]. Be sure your lips glide from a wide open position to a closed one or the pure vowel [a] might result.

EXAMPLES: If you say [a] instead of [aʊ]:   **pound** will sound like **pond.**
down   will sound like **Don.**

[aʊ] is always represented by the letter *o* followed by *u, w,* or *ugh.* **You won't have d<u>ou</u>bts ab<u>ou</u>t the s<u>ou</u>nd** [aʊ]**!**

EXERCISE A

The following words should all be pronounced with [aʊ]. Repeat them carefully after your teacher or the instructor on the tape.

[aʊ] At the Beginning	[aʊ] In the Middle	[aʊ] At the End
owl	loud	cow
out	down	how
hour	crowd	now
ounce	mouse	allow
outlet	vowel	plough

[aʊ] Spelled:

"ou"	"ow"
foul	town
sour	crown
cloud	power
thousand	eyebrow
announce	somehow

A less frequent spelling pattern for [aʊ] consists of the letters *ough*.

EXAMPLES: bough   drought   plough

EXERCISE B

Read the following word pairs aloud. When producing the [aʊ] words be sure to glide your articulators from [a] to [ʊ]. **This exercise is not on the tape.**

[aʊ]	[a]
bound	bond
pound	pond
shout	shot
proud	prod
doubt	dot

Repeat the following phrases and sentences after your teacher or the instructor on the tape. The boldface words should be pronounced with the diphthong [aʊ].

1. **How** are you?
2. **How about** it?
3. **Count** me **out**!

4. I **doubt** it!
5. **hour** after **hour**
6. **around** the **house**

7. **Pronounce** the **vowel sounds**.
8. Don't **shout out loud** in the **house**.
9. The ball **bounced out** of **bounds**.
10. **Howard** is **proud** of his **town**.

SELF-TEST I   (Correct answers may be found in Appendix II on p. 300.)

Read each series of four words out loud. Circle the **ONE** word in each group of four that is **NOT** pronounced with [aʊ]. **This self-test is not on the tape.**

EXAMPLE:	bounce	round	found	(would)
1.	brown	down	flow	frown
2.	foul	group	shout	loud
3.	know	how	now	cow
4.	sour	hour	tour	our
5.	could	count	crown	crowd
6.	thought	plough	drought	thousand
7.	ounce	out	own	ouch
8.	flounder	flood	flour	pounce
9.	allow	about	power	arose
10.	noun	consonant	vowel	sound

Read the following dialogue aloud. Circle all words that should be pronounced with the diphthong [aʊ]. **This self-test is not on the tape.**

· ·

MR. BROWN:	You look (**out**)of sorts. (**How**)come?
MRS. BROWN:	I'm tired out. Didn't you hear the loud noise outside all night?
MR. BROWN:	I didn't hear a sound. I was "out like a light!"
MRS. BROWN:	Our neighbors had a big crowd; they were shouting and howling!
MR. BROWN:	Why didn't you tell them to stop clowning around?
MRS. BROWN:	I didn't want to sound like a grouch.
MR. BROWN:	Next time I'll go out. I'm not afraid to open my mouth!
MRS. BROWN:	I knew I could count on you. Here comes our noisy neighbor Mr. Crowley, right now.
MR. BROWN:	That 300-pound "powerhouse!" Sorry dear, I have to go downtown, NOW!!
MRS. BROWN:	Come back, you coward!!!

· ·

After checking your answers in Appendix II, practice reading the dialogue again.

FOR AN ENCORE ·

Conversation

Start a conversation using as many **"HOW"** questions as you can think of. (**How** do you do? **How** are you? **How's** the weather **out**side? etc.)

PRACTICE [aʊ] OUT LOUD AND . . .

⟨⟨YOU WON'T HAVE DOUBTS ABOUT THE SOUND [aʊ]!⟩⟩

[aɪ] as in *I*, *MY*, and *PIE*
(DICTIONARY MARK: ī)

PRONOUNCING [aɪ]

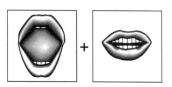

LIPS:	**glide from an open to a slightly parted position.**
JAW:	**rises with the tongue and closes.**
TONGUE:	**glides from low to high near the roof of the mouth.**

[aɪ] is a diphthong. It begins with [a] and ends with [ɪ].

POSSIBLE PRONUNCIATION PROBLEMS

The diphthong [aɪ] should be quite easy for you to pronounce in English. Just be careful of irregular spelling patterns. Remember that [aɪ] is frequently represented by the letters *i* or *y*.

EXAMPLES: ̲ice   m ̲y

Keep trying. Your [aɪ] ***will be quite fine.***

EXERCISE A

The following words should all be pronounced with [aɪ]. Carefully repeat them after your teacher or the instructor on the tape.

[aɪ] At the Beginning	[aɪ] In the Middle	[aɪ] At the End
eye	bite	by
ice	five	cry
I'm	mind	die
I've	sign	tie
item	fight	lie

[aɪ] Spelled:

"i"	"y"	"ie"	"igh"
I	my	die	high
ice	fly	pie	sight
fire	why	tie	night
bite	type	cries	delight
nice	style	fried	frighten

> **HINTS:**
> a. The letter *i* followed by *gh, ld,* or *nd* is usually pronounced [aɪ].
>
> EXAMPLES: si<u>gh</u>t wi<u>ld</u> fi<u>nd</u>
>
> b. When *i* is in a syllable ending in silent *e*, the letter *i* is pronounced [aɪ] (the same name as the alphabet letter i!!!).
>
> EXAMPLES: b<u>i</u>te f<u>i</u>ne ref<u>i</u>nement conf<u>i</u>ne

EXERCISE B

Read the following phrases and sentences aloud. The boldface words should be pronounced with the diphthong [aɪ]. **This exercise is not on the tape.**

1. **Hi**!
2. **Nice** to meet you.
3. **I'm fine**.

4. What **time** is it?
5. **Nice try**!
6. **Rise** and **shine**!

7. The store is open from **nine** to **five**.
8. **I'll buy** the **item** if the **price** is **right**.
9. **I'll try** to **type** it **by tonight**.
10. **My driver's license expires** in **July**.

SELF-TEST I   (Correct answers may be found in Appendix II on p. 301.)

Read each series of four words out loud. Circle the **ONE** word in each group of four that is **NOT** pronounced with [aɪ]. **This self-test is not on the tape.**

EXAMPLE:	pie	line	(rich)	rice
1.	price	crime	pity	pile
2.	mind	kind	spinning	finding
3.	sign	high	fright	freight
4.	list	cite	aisle	cried
5.	gyp	bye	cry	reply
6.	niece	nice	knife	night
7.	style	failed	filed	fire
8.	pretty	try	resign	goodbye
9.	ice cream	eye	aim	aisle
10.	flight	fine	duty	dying

Read the following dialogue aloud. Circle all words that should be pronounced with the diphthong [aɪ]. **This self-test is not on the tape.**

••

MIKE: (Hi,)(Myra!) It's (nice) to see you.
MYRA: Likewise, Mike. How are you?
MIKE: I'm tired. I just came in on a night flight from Ireland.
MYRA: What time did your flight arrive?
MIKE: I arrived at five forty-five in the morning.
MYRA: I'm surprised the airlines have a late night flight.
MIKE: If you don't mind, Myra, I think I'll go home and rest for a while. I'm really "wiped out!"
MYRA: It's quite all right. Goodbye, Mike!

••

After checking your answers in Appendix II, practice reading the dialogue again.

FOR AN ENCORE ·

Reading

Before going to a movie, read the movie guide in your newspaper. Underline all the [aɪ] words in the titles of the movies being advertised. Practice reading the titles out loud.

KEEP TRYING!!!
⟨⟨YOUR [aɪ] WILL BE QUITE FINE.⟩⟩

[ɔɪ] as in *OIL, NOISE,* and *BOY*
(DICTIONARY MARK: oi)

PRONOUNCING [ɔɪ]

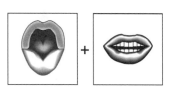

LIPS: glide from a tense oval shape to a relaxed, slightly parted position.

JAW: rises with the tongue and closes.

TONGUE: glides from a low position to high near the roof of the mouth.

[ɔɪ] is a diphthong. It begins with [ɔ] and ends with [ɪ].

POSSIBLE PRONUNCIATION PROBLEMS

You shouldn't have ANY problem at all with the diphthong [ɔɪ]. Its pronunciation will be simple for you. English words with this diphthong are spelled with *oy* or *oi*. There are virtually no exceptions to this rule! ***You'll enjoy pronouncing* [ɔɪ].**

EXERCISE A

The following words should all be pronounced with [ɔɪ]. Repeat them as accurately as possible after your teacher or the instructor on the tape.

[ɔɪ] At the Beginning	[ɔɪ] In the Middle	[ɔɪ] At the End
oil	join	toy
oink	foil	boy
oily	coin	joy
oyster	avoid	enjoy
ointment	noise	annoy

EXERCISE B

Read aloud the following words. Be sure to produce **BOTH** vowel sounds in each diphthong. **This exercise is not on the tape.**

[aʊ]	[aɪ]	[ɔɪ]
foul	file	foil
bow	buy	boy
towel	tile	toil
sow	sigh	soy
owl	aisle	oil

EXERCISE C

Repeat the following phrases, questions, and answers aloud. The boldface words should all be pronounced with [ɔɪ]. Fill in the blanks with your own words. **This exercise is not on the tape.**

1. girls and **boys**
2. flip a **coin**
3. Don't **annoy** me!
4. **Enjoy** yourself.
5. Lower your **voice**.

6. Do you like **broiled** or **boiled oysters**?
   I like _____ _____.

7. Do you need **oil** or **foil**?
   I need _____.

8. Did you buy **choice sirloin** or pork **loin**?
   I bought _____.

9. Are **noisy** children **annoying** or **enjoyable**?
   Noisy children are _____.

10. Would you **enjoy** a trip to **Detroit** or **St. Croix**?
    I'd **enjoy** going to _____!

Read each four-word series aloud. Circle the **ONE** word in each group that is **NOT** pronounced with [ɔɪ]. **This self-test is not on the tape.**

EXAMPLE:	joy	join	enjoy	(jaunt)
1.	voice	avoid	void	vows
2.	noise	nose	hoist	annoy
3.	towel	toy	toil	spoil
4.	Detroit	Illinois	St. Croix	New York
5.	oil	oily	foil	owl
6.	boil	broil	bow	boy
7.	poison	pounce	point	appoint
8.	poise	Joyce	Joan	soil
9.	coil	coal	coy	coin
10.	lobster	sirloin	oyster	moist

FOR AN ENCORE . . . .

Conversation

Whenever you must schedule an appointment with someone (your doctor, lawyer, hairdresser, teacher, etc.) use the phrase *"I'd like to make an* ***appointment*** *with* _____*."* Be sure to pronounce [ɔɪ] correctly.

⟨⟨YOU'LL ENJ<u>OY</u> PRONOUNCING [ɔɪ]!⟩⟩

INTRODUCING STRESS, RHYTHM, AND INTONATION

Thus far, you have been studying the individual sounds of English. These sounds can be significantly affected by vocal features known as *stress, rhythm,* and *intonation*. These vocal features help to convey meaning and must be used correctly if you are to be completely understood.

STRESS is the first vocal feature we will deal with. Speakers must stress certain syllables in words; otherwise the words would be misunderstood or sound strange. For example, improperly placed stress when pronouncing **in**valid (a chronically ill or disabled person) may make it sound like in**val**id (null; legally ineffective). Stress can also change the meaning of a sentence. "**I** saw a movie" is different from "I saw a **movie**." In English, proper use of stress enables you to clearly understand the difference between such words as the noun **pres**ent (gift) and the verb pre**sent** (to introduce; to offer). "**He** won't go" implies a meaning different from "He won't **go**."

RHYTHM is the second feature we will present. Rhythm is created by the strong stresses or beats in a sentence. In many languages, the rhythm is syllable timed. This means that all vowels in all syllables are pronounced almost equally. Syllables are rarely lost or reduced as they are in English. For example, a three-word phrase in *your* language is not likely to become two words. In English, "ham and eggs" is squeezed into two words, "ham'n eggs."

This reduction results because English has a stress-timed rhythm. This means that its rhythm is determined by the number of stresses and not by the number of syllables. English speakers slow down and emphasize heavily stressed words or syllables. They speed up and reduce unstressed ones. For example, the five-word phrase "I will see you tomorrow" may become "I'll seeya t'morrow."

INTONATION is the final vocal feature you will learn about. Intonation patterns involve pitch and are responsible for the melody of the language. Speakers frequently depend more on intonation patterns to convey their meaning than on the pronunciation of individual vowels and consonants. For example, in English, the same words can be used to make a statement or ask a question. If your vocal intonation rises, you are asking a question "He speaks English?" If your voice falls, you are making a statement "He speaks English." The sentence "That's Bill's car" becomes the question "That's Bill's car?" when you raise the pitch of your voice at the end.

So—now you can appreciate the common expression, **It's not WHAT you say, it's HOW you say it!**

Although your English grammar may be perfect and you can pronounce individual sounds correctly, you will still have a noticeable foreign accent until you master the **stress, rhythm,** and **intonation** patterns of English.

STRESS WITHIN THE WORD

DEFINITION

Stress refers to the amount of volume that a speaker gives to a particular sound, syllable, or word while saying it. Stressed sounds and syllables are **louder** and longer than unstressed ones. The words *accent*, *stress,* and *emphasis* are frequently used interchangeably.

STRESS IN ENGLISH

A major characteristic of the English language is the use of strong and weak stress. Every word of more than one syllable has a syllable that is emphasized more than the others. Accented syllables receive more force and are **louder** than unaccented ones. Correct use of stress is essential for achieving proper pronunciation of words.

POSSIBLE PRONUNCIATION PROBLEMS

Many languages have specific rules for accenting words. When there is an exception to the rule, an accent mark is generally written above the stressed syllable. There are **NO** consistent rules in English. Consequently, you may have difficulty when attempting to accent syllables correctly.

1. You may place the stress on the **wrong** syllable.

   EXAMPLES: **désert**   would sound like **dessért**
   ínvalid   would sound like **inválid**

2. You may stress every vowel in a word equally and forget to reduce vowels in unaccented syllables (refer back to page 203).

   EXAMPLES: **tomórrow** would sound like **tómórrów**
   becáuse   would sound like **bécáuse**

As you practice imitating your teacher or the instructor on the tapes, your ability to use proper stress patterns when speaking English will improve. ***BE POSITIVE AND KEEP PRACTICING!***

WORDS STRESSED ON THE FIRST SYLLABLE

I. The majority of two-syllable words are accented on the FIRST syllable.

EXAMPLES: Tuésday áwful éver bróther óven wíndow

II. Compound nouns are usually accented on the FIRST syllable.

EXAMPLES: bédroom aírfield stóplight schoólhouse boókstore

III. Numbers that are multiples of ten are accented on the FIRST syllable.

EXAMPLES: twénty thírty fórty fífty síxty séventy

WORDS STRESSED ON THE SECOND SYLLABLE

I. Reflexive pronouns are usually accented on the SECOND syllable.

EXAMPLES: mysélf yoursélf himsélf hersélf oursélves

II. Compound verbs are usually accented on the SECOND or LAST syllable.

EXAMPLES: outdóne outsmárt outdó outrún overloók overcóme

EXERCISE A

Repeat the following words as accurately as possible after your teacher or the instructor on the tape. Be sure to stress the **first** syllable of the words in column I and the **second** syllable of the words in column II.

Stress on the FIRST Syllable	Stress on the SECOND Syllable
ápple	aróund
táble	allów
móther	invíte
téacher	compléte
wínter	suppórt

EXERCISE B

The following three-syllable words have a variety of stress patterns. Repeat them as accurately as possible after your teacher or the instructor on the tape. **Remember** to EMPHASIZE the stressed syllable.

Primary stress on the FIRST SYLLABLE	Primary stress on the SECOND SYLLABLE	Primary stress on the THIRD SYLLABLE
áccident	accéptance	afternoón
stráwberry	vanílla	absolúte
séventy	exámine	seventeén
yésterday	tomórrow	recomménd
président	políceman	guaranteé

STRESS IN NOUN/VERB PAIRS

There are many nouns and verbs that are the same in the written form. We can distinguish between these word pairs in their spoken form through the use of stress. In these pairs, the noun will always be stressed on the first syllable, the verb on the second syllable.

EXERCISE C

Repeat the following noun/verb pairs after your teacher or the instructor on the tape. Remember to stress the **noun** on the FIRST syllable and **verb** on the SECOND.

Nouns

cónflict   (controversy)
cónduct   (one's behavior)
cóntent   (subject matter)
désert   (barren region)
dígest   (synopsis)
cóntest   (competition)
pérmit   (written warrant)
éxploit   (notable act, adventure)
óbject   (material thing)
íncrease (enlargement)

Verbs

conflíct (to clash)
condúct   (to lead or guide)
contént   (to satisfy)
desért   (to abandon)
digést   (to absorb)
contést   (to dispute or challenge)
permít   (to allow or consent)
explóit   (to take advantage of)
objéct   (to oppose or disagree)
increáse (to make larger)

 # EXERCISE D

Repeat the following sentences as accurately as possible after your teacher or the instructor on the tape. Carefully pronounce the stress pattern differences between the boldface words in each sentence.

1. Please **recórd** the **récord**.
2. She was **complétely cómpetent**.
3. We **projéct** that the **próject** will be good.
4. The Sheik was **fífty** with **fifteén** wives!
5. His hairline began **recéding récently**.
6. The teacher was **contént** with the **cóntent** of the report.
7. He **objécts** to the **óbjects**.
8. I **mistrúst Míster** Smith.
9. She will **presént** you with a **présent**.
10. I **suppóse súpper** will be served.

EXERCISE E

Read the following dialogue aloud. Pay careful attention to the stress patterns of the various nouns and verbs in boldface type. **This exercise is not on the tape.**

....

MICHAEL: Welcome to the annual meeting of the **Pérry Próduce Cómpany**. Does **éveryone** remember our **mótto?**

ALL: Yes. "We **prodúce** the best **próduce!**"

MICHAEL: Thomas, do you think there will be an **íncrease** in **prófits** next year?

THOMAS: Yes, Michael. We will **increáse** our **prófits**. **Prógress** is our goal!

MICHAEL: Do you **projéct** having a new **márket?**

THOMAS: Yes. Our latest **próject** is the **ímport** of **exótic** fruit.

MICHAEL: **Re´ally!** What will we **impórt?**

THOMAS: **Píneapple** from **Hawáii** and dates from the Sahara **Désert**.

MICHAEL: Did you say **désert** or **dessért?** I love **dessérts!**

THOMAS: OK, Mike. I'm so **contént** with the **cóntent** of this **me´eting**, I'll treat you to some fresh fruit.

MICHAEL: Please, Tom, no more fruit! *Health* **Dígest** says fruit is hard to **digést**. I'll have **stráwberry íce cream!**

....

Practice the dialogue out loud using proper stress patterns.

SELF-TEST I (Correct answers may be found in Appendix II on p. 302.)

Pronounce the following words aloud. Circle the syllable that receives primary stress. **This self-test is not on the tape.**

EXAMPLE: collecting   col (lect) ing

1. themselves   them   selves
2. birthday   birth   day
3. engineer   en   gi   neer
4. September   Sep   tem   ber
5. Saturday   Sat   ur   day

SELF-TEST II   (Correct answers may be found in Appendix II on p. 302.)

Listen carefully to your teacher or the tape as the following groups of words are presented. Circle the **one** word in each group that has a different stress pattern than the others.

EXAMPLE: connect   control   contain   (constant)

1.   agent   annoy   allow   agree
2.   upon   until   undo   under
3.   protect   program   pronoun   protein
4.   token   toaster   today   total
5.   supper   sunken   suffer   support

SELF-TEST III   (Correct answers may be found in Appendix II on p. 302.)

Read the following sentences aloud. Circle the number of the stressed sylla-ble in each italicized word. **This self-test is not on the tape.**

EXAMPLE: (①) 2
              The *convict* escaped from jail.

              1 2
1. Keep a *record* of your expenses.
              1 2
2. The police don't *suspect* anyone.
              1 2
3. The student will *present* a speech.
              1 2
4 The *present* was not wrapped.
              1 23
5. The *invalid* was in the hospital.

SELF-TEST IV   (Correct answers may be found in Appendix II on p. 303.)

Repeat the poem on page 232 line by line after your teacher or the instruc-tor on the tape. Circle the number of the stressed syllable in each two-syllable word.

(1) 2   (1) 2 (1) 2
MONEY   by Richard Armour

••

  1 2
Workers earn it,
    1   2
Spendthrifts burn it,
    1 2
Bankers lend it,
    1 2
Women spend it,
    1 2
Forgers fake it,
   1 2
Taxes take it,
  1   2
Dying leave it,
       1 2
Heirs receive it,
  1   2
Thrifty save it,
   1 2
Misers crave it,
  1   2
Robbers seize it,
      1 2
Rich increase it,
   1   2
Gamblers lose it...

I could use it!   (Reprinted by permission of BRANDEN PUBLISHING, Boston)
••

After checking your answers in Appendix II, recite the poem again using proper stress patterns. Observe how your teacher or the instructor on the tape consistently emphasizes the noun in each line.

STRESS WITHIN THE SENTENCE

SENTENCE STRESS IN ENGLISH

You have already learned that word stress is a major feature of English. Stress patterns go beyond the word level. Just as it is awkward sounding to stress the syllables in a word incorrectly or to stress them all equally, it is unnatural sounding to stress all the words in a sentence equally or improperly. Effective use of strong and weak emphasis in phrases and sentences will help you achieve your goal of sounding like a native English speaker.

POSSIBLE PRONUNCIATION PROBLEMS

English sentence level stress patterns may not be used the same way as in your language. In English, specific words within a sentence are emphasized or spoken louder to make them stand out. (*"It's not **HIS** house; it's **HER** house."*) Your language frequently uses its grammar instead of word stress to convey the same meaning. Consequently, you may be confused about when to use strong stress (and when not to use it!) in English sentences. Using the stress patterns of your native language will contribute to your foreign accent.

1. You may place the stress on the wrong word. This could:

   a. Completely change the meaning of your statement.

   EXAMPLE: *"He lives in the green **house**"* would sound like *"He lives in the **green**house."*

   b. Distort your intended meaning of the sentence.

   EXAMPLE: *"**STEVE'S** my cousin" (not Sam)* would sound like *"Steve's my **COUSIN**" (not my brother).*

2. You may be giving too much or equal stress to unimportant or "function words."

> EXAMPLE: *"I'm in the **HOUSE**"* would sound like *"I'm **IN THE** house."*
>
> *"He's at the **STORE**"* would sound like ***"HE'S AT THE STORE."***

After reading the explanations and listening to the tape a few times, you will begin to understand the use of English stress patterns. ***YOU SHOULD BE VERY PROUD OF YOURSELF. YOU'VE ALREADY COME A LONG WAY!***

WORDS GENERALLY STRESSED IN SENTENCES: CONTENT WORDS

Content words are the important words in a sentence which convey meaning. We normally **STRESS** content words when speaking. Content words include all the major parts of speech such as nouns, verbs, adjectives, adverbs, and question words.

WORDS GENERALLY UNSTRESSED IN SENTENCES: FUNCTION WORDS

Function words are the unimportant words in a sentence. They don't carry as much meaning as content words. We normally do **NOT** stress function words when speaking. Function words include the following parts of speech:

a. articles   *(the, a)*
b. prepositions   *(for, of, in, to)*
c. pronouns   *(I, her, him, he, she, you)*
d. conjunctions *(but, as, and)*
e. helping verbs *(is, was, are, were, has, can)*

EXERCISE A

Repeat the following common expressions after your teacher or the instructor on the tape. Be sure to **STRESS** the content words and **NOT** the function words.

1. in a **moment**
2. to **tell** the **truth**
3. **Silence** is **golden**!
4. **Honesty** is the **best policy**.
5. A **penny saved** is a **penny earned**.

STRESSING WORDS TO CLARIFY OR CHANGE MEANING

Sometimes a speaker wants his or her sentence to convey a special meaning which it wouldn't have in the written form. This can be done by stressing a specific word in order to call attention to it. The word that receives the stress depends on the personal motive of the speaker.

EXAMPLE A: "I **BOUGHT** ten ties." (I wasn't *given* the ties; I **bought** them.)
EXAMPLE B: "I bought ten **TIES**." (I didn't buy *shirts*; I bought **ties**.)

EXERCISE B

The boldface words in the following questions and responses should receive more emphasis than the others. Repeat them after your teacher or the instructor on the tape.

1. **Who** likes candy?   **Sam** likes candy.
2. **What** does Sam like?   Sam likes **candy**.
3. Is that **his** car?   No, that's **her** car.
4. Will she **stay**?   No, she'll **leave**.
5. **Where** are you going?   I'm going **home.**
6. **Who's** going home?   **I'm** going home.
7. **When** are you going home? I'm going home **now**.
8. Did Mary buy a **book**?   No, she bought a **pen**.
9. Did **Mary** buy a book?   No, **Sue** bought a book.
10. Did Mary **buy** a book?   No, Mary **borrowed** a book.

STRESS IN ADJECTIVE/NOUN COMBINATIONS

When you speak, it's important to use words that describe what you are talking about. Words that describe nouns (people, places or things) are called *adjectives*. When you use adjective/noun combinations, the noun normally receives greater stress.

EXAMPLES: big **DÓG**   good **BOÓK**   pretty **DRÉSS**   nice **BÓY**

By accidentally stressing the adjective, you might mistakenly say a compound noun with a completely different meaning. Your listeners will be confused!

If you stress the adjective instead of the noun:

a. the *green **house***   becomes the ***green**house*

b. the *dark **room***   becomes the ***dark**room*

EXERCISE C

Read the following sentence pairs containing adjective/noun combinations and compound words aloud. Be sure to STRESS the NOUN in the sentences in column 1. **This exercise is not on the tape.**

Sentences with Adjective/Noun Combinations	Sentences with Compound Nouns
The *blue **bird*** is pretty.	The ***blue**bird* is pretty.
We live in the white ***house***.	We live in the **White** House.
It's in the *dark **room***.	It's in the ***dark**room*.
He caught a white ***fish***.	He caught a ***white**fish*.
Look at the *black **bird***.	Look at the ***black**bird*.

EXERCISE D

Read the following dialogue aloud. Pay careful attention to the sentence stress patterns suggested. **This exercise is not on the tape.**

. . . .

JOHN: Anne, who was on the **phone**?

ANNE: My old friend **Mary**.

JOHN: Mary **Jones**?

ANNE: No. Mary **Hall**.

JOHN: I don't know Mary **Hall**. Where is she **from**?

ANNE: She's from **Washington**.

JOHN: Washington the **state** or Washington the **city**?

ANNE: Washington, D.C., our nation's **capital**.

JOHN: Is that where she **lives**?

ANNE: Yes, she still lives in the white **house**.

JOHN: The **White** House? With the **President**?

ANNE: No, silly. The white **house** on **First** street.

JOHN: What did she **want**?

ANNE: She wants to **come** here.

JOHN: Come **here? When**?

ANNE: In a **week**. She's bringing her black **bird,** her **collie,** her **snakes,** her . . .

JUAN: **Stop!**   She's bringing a **zoo** to **our** house?

ANNA: No, John. She's opening a **pet** store here in **town**.

. . . .

SELF-TEST I   (Correct answers may be found in Appendix II on p. 303.)

Read the following sentences aloud. Circle all *content words* and underline all *function words*. **This self-test is not on the tape.**

EXAMPLE: The (dogs) are (barking.)

1. Mary is a good friend.
2. Steve is tall and handsome.
3. It's early in the morning.
4. The baby caught a cold.
5. I ate a piece of pie.
6. The store opens at nine.
7. My shoes hurt my feet.
8. Please look for the book.
9. He's leaving in a week.
10. We walked in the snow.

....

After checking your answers in Appendix II, read the sentences again. Be sure to **stress** all *content words* and **unstress** all *function words*.

 ## SELF-TEST II   (Correct answers may be found in Appendix II on p. 304.)

Your teacher or the instructor on the tape will say EITHER the adjective/noun combination **OR** the compound noun in each of the following pairs. Listen carefully and circle the choice that you hear.

EXAMPLE A: dark **room**   **dárk**room
EXAMPLE B: green **hoúse**   **green**house

1. black **bird**   **black**bird
2. copper **head**   **copper**head
3. blue **bell**   **blue**bell
4. light **house**   **light**house
5. white **house**   **White** House

SELF-TEST III   (Correct answers may be found in Appendix II on p. 304.)

In each of the following sentences, the unimportant or *function words* have been omitted. Fill in the blanks with appropriate *function words*. **This self-test is not on the tape.**

EXAMPLE: I went *to the* store.

1. Mary wants ____ cup ____ coffee.
2. ____ show started ____ eight.
3. ____ movie ____ very funny.
4. Sue ate ____ slice ____ cake.
5. We met ____ couple ____ friends ____ mine.

After checking your answers in Appendix II, practice reading the sentences aloud. Remember, **DO NOT** stress the *function words!*

SELF-TEST IV   (Correct answers may be found in Appendix II on p. 304.)

Read the following sentences aloud. One word in each sentence should be stressed more than the others. Circle the word that you must stress to clarify the intended meaning of the sentence. Refer back to Exercise D if necessary. **This self-test is not on the tape.**

EXAMPLE A: Mary (Hall) will visit John and Anne. (Not Mary Jones.)

EXAMPLE B: Mary is from (Washington) (She isn't from New York.)

  1. Mary is Anne's friend. (She isn't her cousin.)
  2. John is married to Anne. (They aren't engaged anymore.)
  3. She's from Washington, D.C. (She's not from Washington state.)
  4. She lives in the white house. (She doesn't live in the White House.)
  5. Her house is on First Street. (It isn't on First Avenue.)
  6. Anne and John got married three years ago. (Not five years ago.)
  7. They own a small home. (They don't rent.)
  8. Mary wants to come in a week. (She doesn't want to wait a month.)
  9. She'll bring her collie and snakes. (She's not bringing her poodle.)
10. Mary is opening a pet store. (Not a toy store.)

We hope this chapter on stress didn't cause you any stress! You did a beautiful job! It's time to take a break and **RELAX** for a while. When you're well rested, move on to the next chapter.
You'll soon get the RHYTHM!!! ⟶

RHYTHM

RHYTHM IN ENGLISH

The rhythm of conversational English is more rapid and less precise than formal speech. Every spoken sentence contains syllables or words that receive primary stress. Like the beats in music, strong stresses occur regularly to create a rhythm. Certain words within the sentence must be emphasized while others are spoken more rapidly. This frequently causes sounds to be reduced, changed, or completely omitted. To keep the sentence flowing, words are linked together into phrases and separated by pauses to convey meaning clearly. Effective use of rhythm will help you to achieve more natural-sounding speech.

POSSIBLE PRONUNCIATION PROBLEMS

In many languages, all vowels in all syllables are pronounced almost equally. Syllables are rarely lost or reduced as they are in English. It is likely that you are using your language's conversational rhythm patterns when speaking English. This habit will contribute to a noticeable foreign accent.

1. You may stress each word equally or too precisely.

   EXAMPLE: *"He will **léave** at **thrée**"* would sound like "**Hé wíll léave át thrée.**"

2. You may avoid the use of contractions or reduced forms.

   EXAMPLES: *"I **can't** go"* would sound like *"I **cannot** go."*

   *"He likes **ham'n eggs**"* would sound like *"He likes **ham and eggs.**"*

3. You may insert phrases incorrectly between the words of the sentence, and these will obscure meaning and create a faulty rhythm.

   EXAMPLE: *"I don't know Joan"* would sound like *"I don't know, Joan."*

We know this can be slightly confusing at first. *Please do not be concerned! THE EXERCISES IN THIS CHAPTER WILL GET YOU RIGHT INTO THE RHYTHM!!!*

CONTRACTIONS

Contractions are two words that are combined together to form one. Contractions are used frequently in spoken English and are grammatically correct. If you use the full form of the contraction in conversation, your speech will sound stilted and unnatural.

EXAMPLES: | *Contraction* | *Full Form* |
| --- | --- |
| I'll | I will |
| you're | you are |
| he's | he is |
| we've | we have |
| isn't | is not |

EXERCISE A

Read the following pairs of sentences aloud. The first sentence is written in full form, the second contains the contraction. Observe how smooth and natural the second sentence sounds compared with the choppy rhythm of the first sentence. **This exercise is not on the tape.**

1. I am late again.	I'm late again.
2. Mary does not know.	Mary doesn't know.
3. You are next in line.	You're next in line.
4. We have already met.	We've already met.
5. That is right!	That's right!
6. They will not sing.	They won't sing.
7. Steve has not eaten.	Steve hasn't eaten.
8. He is very nice.	He's very nice.
9. Please do not yell.	Please don't yell.
10. We will be there.	We'll be there.

LINKING AND WORD REDUCTIONS

In conversational English, the words in phrases and short sentences should be linked together as if they were one word.

EXAMPLE A: *"How are you?"* should be pronounced *"Howareyou?"*
EXAMPLE B: *"Do it now!"* should be pronounced *"Doitnow!"*

When words are linked together in this manner, sounds are frequently reduced or omitted completely. (The linking of words and the reductions and omissions of sounds occur **ONLY** in conversational speech. *They are **never** written.)*

EXAMPLE A: *"I miss Sam"* = *"I misam."*
EXAMPLE B: *"Don't take it."* = *"Don'take it."*

This style of speaking (the use of **contractions, linking,** and **word reductions**) is used by American English speakers in normal conversation and is perfectly acceptable spoken language. Try to use these forms as often as possible when speaking English. ***YOU'LL SOON GET THE RHYTHM!!!***

EXERCISE B

Repeat the following phrases and sentences after your teacher or the instructor on the tape. Be sure to blend the words together smoothly and to use reduced forms appropriately.

1. cream'n sugar   (cream and sugar)
2. bread'n butter   (bread and butter)
3. ham'n cheese   (ham and cheese)
4. pieceəpie   (piece of pie)
5. I gotə school   (I go to school)

SOUND CHANGES

The rapid speech of native American English speakers can be difficult for you to understand at times. Sounds in words may run together, disappear, or actually change.

EXAMPLES: *"When did you see her?"* might sound like *"Whenja see-er?"*
"I'll meet you" might sound like *"I'll meetcha."*

It's true that such expressions are not the *"King's English."* In fact, the king would probably turn over in his grave if he were to hear them! Nevertheless, American English speakers use such rhythm patterns in informal, rapid speech. It is important for you to be able to understand these expressions when you hear them.

EXERCISE C

Listen carefully to your teacher or the tape as the following commonly used expressions are presented using the rapid, informal rhythm. (The slow, careful speech form is provided to help you *"SEE"* as well as *"HEAR"* the difference!)

1. Whatsidoin?   (What is he doing?)
2. Whenjarive?   (When did you arrive?)
3. Saniceday!   (It's a nice day!)
4. Nicetəmeetchə   (Nice to meet you.)
5. Whervyəbeen?   (Where have you been?)

DOUBLE CONSONANTS

Many words in English are spelled with the same two consecutive consonant letters (for example, "li<u>tt</u>le" or "co<u>ff</u>ee"). Pronouncing the same sound twice will disrupt your rhythm of spoken English and contribute to your accent.

EXAMPLE A: **pretty** [prɪtɪ]   will sound like **pret-ty**.
EXAMPLE B: **happen** [hæpən] will sound like **hap-pen**.

EXERCISE D

Read the following words aloud. Be sure to pronounce the identical consonant letters in each word as **ONE** sound. **This exercise is not on the tape.**

1. trigger	6. happy	11. little
2. coffee	7. penny	12. passing
3. fussy	8. offer	13. butter
4. silly	9. parrot	14. pillow
5. cotton	10. paddle	15. traffic

PHRASING AND PAUSING

A **phrase** is a thought group or a group of words that convey meaning. A **pause** is a brief moment during which the speaker is silent. Sentences should be divided into phrases or thought groups through the use of pauses. The speaker can use a pause to convey or emphasize meaning or simply to take a breath!

EXERCISE E

Read the following sentences aloud. Be sure to PAUSE between each phrase marked by the slanted lines and to blend the words in each phrase. **This exercise is not on the tape.**

1. The phone book // is on the shelf.
2. Steve said // "Sue is gone."
3. "Please help me // Sally."
4. Mr. White // our neighbor // is very nice.
5. I don't agree // and I won't change my mind.

SELF-TEST I

(Correct answers may be found in Appendix II on p.304.)

Read the following sentences aloud. Fill in the blanks with the correct contraction. **This self-test is not on the tape.**

EXAMPLE A: **_He's_** my favorite teacher. (He is)
EXAMPLE B: **_We're_** good friends. (We are)

1. _____ a student. (I am)
2. Lynn _____ play tennis. (does not)
3. _____ seen that movie. (We have)
4. _____ quite right. (You are)
5. His brother _____ come. (cannot)
6. He _____ arrived yet. (has not)
7. _____ be ten minutes late. (We will)
8. I don't think _____ coming with us. (they are)
9. My son _____ there. (was not)
10. My car _____ ready yet. (is not)

SELF-TEST II

(Correct answers may be found in Appendix II on p. 305.)

Read the following sentences aloud, pausing where indicated. Underline the sentence in each pair that is correctly marked for pauses. **This self-test is not on the tape.**

EXAMPLE: I finished my homework // and watched TV.
         I finished // my homework and watched TV.

1. Meet me at the bus stop // after you're done.
   Meet me at the bus // stop after you're done.

2. Bill Brown the mayor will // speak tonight.
   Bill Brown // the mayor // will speak tonight.

3. Please clean your room // before leaving.
   Please clean your // room before leaving.

4. The truth is I don't // like it.
   The truth is // I don't like it.

5. He was there // for the first time.
   He was there for // the first time.

6. Charles Dickens // the famous author // wrote *David Copperfield*.
   Charles Dickens the famous author wrote // *David Copperfield*.

7. Where there's a will // there's a way.
   Where there's a // will there's a // way.

8. Do unto others as // you would have them do // unto you.
   Do unto others // as you would have them // do unto you.

9. Patrick Henry said // "Give me liberty // or give me death."
   Patrick Henry // said "Give me // liberty or give me death."

10. When in Rome do // as the Romans do.
    When in Rome // do as the Romans do.

After checking your answers in Appendix II, reread the underlined sentences. Be sure to pause between each phrase marked by the slanted lines and to blend the words in each phrase.

INTONATION

DEFINITION

Intonation refers to the use of melody and the rise and fall of the voice when speaking. Each language uses rising and falling pitches differently and has its own distinctive melody and intonation patterns. In fact, babies usually recognize and use the intonation of their native language before they learn actual speech sounds and words.

INTONATION IN ENGLISH

Intonation can determine grammatical meaning as well as the speaker's attitude. It will "tell" whether a person is making a statement or asking a question; it will also indicate if the person is confident, doubtful, shy, annoyed, or impatient. Correct use of intonation is necessary to convey your message correctly and to make you sound like a native English speaker.

POSSIBLE PRONUNCIATION PROBLEMS

English has several basic intonation contours. However, there are many more intonational variations which change with a speaker's intended meaning, attitude, and emotional state of mind. Without realizing it, you can confuse your listener by using incorrect English intonation patterns.

1. Your voice might stay level when it should rise or fall. This would:

   a. Make you sound bored or uninterested.
   b. Confuse your listeners into thinking you didn't finish your sentence or question.

   EXAMPLE: *"I went home,"* would sound like *"I went home . . . and . . ."*

2. Your voice might rise when it should fall. This would:

   a. Change a declarative statement into a question.

   EXAMPLE: *"That's Bill's car."* would sound like *"That's Bill's car?"*

   b. Make you sound doubtful or annoyed.

Listen to the tape several times before trying to imitate the instructor. With practice, you will soon notice great improvement. **KEEP UP THE GOOD WORK!**

PHRASES ENDING WITH A FALLING PITCH

I. Declarative statements

EXAMPLES: Linda is my sister. ↘ He is not going. ↘

II. Questions that require more than a YES/NO response (such question words include *who, what, when, why, where, which, how*)

EXAMPLES: Where is my book? ↘   (On the table. ↘)
When did he leave? ↘   (At three o'clock. ↘)

PHRASES ENDING WITH A RISING PITCH

I. Questions that ask for a YES/NO response (such question words include *can, do, will, would, may, is, etc.*)

EXAMPLES: Will you stay? ↗   (No, I can't. ↘)
Do you like school? ↗   (Yes, I do. ↘)

II. Statements that express doubt or uncertainty

EXAMPLES: I'm not positive. ↗ I think he's coming. ↗

EXERCISE A

Repeat the statements and questions on page 249 after the instructor on the tape. Make your voice **FALL** at the end of each of the sentences and questions. Remember, questions that cannot be answered with yes or no take the same **downward** intonation as declarative statements.

1. I have four brothers. ↘
2. He is not my friend. ↘
3. We like ice cream. ↘
4. Tim bought a new car. ↘
5. She likes to play tennis. ↘
6. What is your name? ↘
7. How is your family? ↘
8. Who will drive you home? ↘
9. Why did he leave? ↘
10. Which book is yours? ↘

EXERCISE B

Repeat the following yes/no questions and sample answers after the instructor on the tape. Be sure your voice **rises** ↗ at the end of each question and **falls** ↘ at the end of each response.

YES/NO Questions ↗	Responses ↘
1. Can you see?	Yes, I can.
2. Does he play golf?	Yes, he does.
3. May I borrow it?	Yes, you may.
4. Will she help?	No, she won't.
5. Did he arrive?	Yes, he's here now.

SOUNDING CONFIDENT INSTEAD OF UNCERTAIN

As was already discussed, a **falling** pitch should be used at the end of declarative statements. It will help you sound confident and sure of yourself. On the other hand, using an **upward** pitch at the end of the same sentences indicates that the speaker is doubtful or uncertain about what he or she is saying.

EXAMPLE: They have 20 children. ↘ (stated as a fact)
They have 20 children. ↗ (stated with doubt or disbelief)

EXERCISE C

Read each of the following statements twice. Use a **falling** ↘ pitch to end the sentences in the first column, and an **upward** ↗ pitch to end the sentences in the second column. *(Notice how the **falling** pitch in the first reading helps you to sound sure of yourself while the **rising** pitch in the second reading makes you sound doubtful or uncertain.)* **This exercise is not on the tape.**

Stated with Certainty ↘	Stated with Doubt ↗
1. He ate 25 hot dogs.	He ate 25 hot dogs.
2. The boss gave him a raise.	The boss gave him a raise.
3. You ran 55 miles.	You ran 55 miles.
4. Mike was elected president.	Mike was elected president.
5. It's already 3 o'clock.	It's already 3 o'clock.

INTONATION IN SENTENCES WITH TWO OR MORE PHRASES

Intonation also tells the listener if a speaker has completed the statement or question, or whether he or she has more to say. Many sentences are spoken with two or more phrases joined together with such connecting words as *and, if, or, so,* or *but.*

EXAMPLES: *He can sing, but he can't dance.*
We were hungry, thirsty, and tired.

If your voice drops after the first phrase, your listener will think you are finished with the sentence. To make it clear that you have more to say, you must keep your voice **level** → before the connecting word and not allow it to **fall** ↘ until you finish your sentence.

EXAMPLES: *He can sing* →*, but he can't dance.* ↘
We were hungry →*, thirsty* →*, and tired.* ↘

I. Declarative sentences with two or more phrases

Keep your voice **level** → before the connecting word and **lower** it at the end.

EXAMPLES: *I must buy coffee* →, *tea* →, *and milk.* ↘
       She speaks French →, *but not Spanish.* ↘

II. Questions presenting two or more choices

This intonation pattern is the same as for declarative sentences with two or more phrases. Keep your voice **level** → before the connecting word and **lower** it when you finish your question. ↘

EXAMPLES: *Would you like cake* →, *or pie?* ↘
       Is he leaving tomorrow →, *or Sunday?* ↘

III. Yes/no questions with two or more phrases

Keep your voice **level** → before the connecting word, and use a **rising** pitch ↗ at the end of your question.

EXAMPLES: *Will you come* → *if I drive you?* ↗
       Did he like the new belt → *and gloves I bought?* ↗

EXERCISE D

Read the following dialogue aloud. Use the correct intonation patterns as indicated by the intonation arrows. **This exercise is not on the tape.**

   ↘ = **Voice falls**   ↗ = **Voice rises**   → = **Voice stays level**

....

HUSBAND: Hi, honey. ↘ What did you do today? ↘
WIFE: I went shopping. ↘
HUSBAND: You went shopping? ↗ Again? ↗
WIFE: Yes. ↘ The store had a big sale. ↘ Everything was half price. ↘
HUSBAND: What did you buy now? ↘

WIFE:	I bought this blouse for thirty dollars. _↘_ Isn't it stunning? _↗_
HUSBAND:	Yes, it's stunning. _↘_ I'm the one that's stunned. _↘_
WIFE:	Do you like the green hat _→_ or the red one? _↘_
HUSBAND:	I like the cheaper one. _↘_
WIFE:	I also bought a belt _→_ , scarf _→_ , dress _→_ , and shoes. _↘_
HUSBAND:	Stop it! _↘_ I'm afraid to hear any more. _↘_ Do we have any money left? _↗_
WIFE:	Yes, dear, we have lots of money left. _↘_ I saved two hundred dollars on my new clothes, so I bought you a set of golf clubs. _↘_
HUSBAND:	Really? _↗_ I always said you were a great shopper! _↘_

• •

SELF-TEST I   (Correct answers may be found in Appendix II on p. 305.)

Listen carefully as the following sentences are presented. The instructor on the tape (or your teacher) will say some of them with certainty and some with doubt, using only intonation to show the difference. On the answer sheet below, circle the sentence you hear.

Sentence #	Stated with Certainty ↘	Stated with Doubt ↗
EXAMPLE A:	*Sam will be ready soon* (circled)	*Sam will be ready soon.*
EXAMPLE B:	*The store is open.*	*The store is open.* (circled)
1.	Ron did 90 sit-ups.	Ron did 90 sit-ups.
2.	It only cost ten cents.	It only cost ten cents.
3.	He's really smart.	He's really smart.
4.	She's been married eight times.	She's been married eight times.
5.	You drank two gallons of wine.	You drank two gallons of wine.

On the line to the right of each of the following statements or questions, draw the correct intonation arrow. (↘ = voice falls; ↗ = voice rises) **This self-test is not on the tape.**

EXAMPLES: *I feel fine.* __↘__ (Declarative sentence)
             Can you sing? __↗__ (Yes/no question)

1. When's your birthday?   _____
2. Did you see my friend?   _____
3. How are you?   _____
4. I'm fine, thank you.   _____
5. Why were you absent?   _____
6. Can you have dinner?   _____
7. I don't like beets.   _____
8. How do you know?   _____
9. Where is the pencil?   _____
10. What is your name?   _____

SELF-TEST III   (Correct answers may be found in Appendix II on p. 306.)

Draw the correct intonation arrows in the blanks of the following multiple-phrase sentences. (__↘__ = voice falls; __→__ = voice level; __↗__ = voice rises.) **This self-test is not on the tape.**

EXAMPLE: *Do you want coffee,* __→__ *tea,* __→__ *or milk?* __↘__

1. We enjoy swimming, _____ hiking, _____ and tennis. _____
2. Is a barbecue all right _____ if it doesn't rain? _____
3. If it rains tomorrow _____ the game is off._____
4. Is he sick? _____ I hope not. _____
5. Please bring me the hammer, _____ nails, _____ and scissors. _____
6. Do you like grapes, _____ pears, _____ and plums? _____
7. May I leave now, _____ or should I wait? _____
8. He's good at math, _____ but not spelling. _____
9. Call me later, _____ if it's not too late. _____
10. Will you visit us _____ if you're in town? _____

FOR AN ENCORE . . . .

Listening

Listen as a native English speaker tells a joke. It may be a television personality or someone you know personally. Observe the speaker's use of vocal melody and intonation patterns which make the joke effective.

Conversation

Practice the joke you heard and analyzed for intonation. Tape yourself saying the joke; be sure to use the proper intonation—*ESPECIALLY ON THE PUNCH LINE!* When you feel confident, tell the joke to three different people.

THAT'S ALL FOLKS!!!

Believe it or not, you have just finished reading the LAST chapter in the book. **CONGRATULATIONS!!** You've earned your degree in **English Pronunciation for International Students.** It was worth all that hard work, wasn't it? **But—*education is a continuing process. Although we've stressed it all along, we'll say it again:* THE MORE YOU PRACTICE, THE BETTER YOU WILL BECOME.**

Daniel Webster once said, *"If all my possessions were taken from me with one exception, I would choose to keep the power of communication, for by it, I would soon regain all the rest."*

SO—keep practicing and CLEAR, EFFECTIVE, COMMUNICATION WILL BE YOURS FOREVER.

Best of luck always,

Lillian Poms

Paulette Dale

Lillian Poms and Paulette Dale

APPENDIX I
TO THE TEACHER

WELCOME TO THE CHALLENGE! You recommended **English Pronunciation for International Students** to your students because you are committed to helping them improve their pronunciation of English. This is a difficult task. But—it's NOT impossible. Teaching and learning English pronunciation can be difficult, tedious work. It can also be more fun than you ever imagined possible! (In our accent reduction classes, there have been countless occasions when we, along with our students, have laughed long and hard enough for tears to roll!)

Some of you are already experienced ESL or speech instructors and/or speech pathologists involved in teaching foreign accent reduction classes, and you already employ a variety of effective techniques with your students. PLEASE—share some of your most successful ones with us. AND—we invite you to let us know how you like OUR suggestions. **We truly look forward to hearing from you!**

Some of you are new at teaching English pronunciation to non-native speakers. **DON'T WORRY!** An enthusiastic attitude and genuine desire to learn with your students will be more valuable than years of experience. As you'll quickly realize, the **English Pronunciation for International Students** program provides you with an easy-to-follow, systematic approach to teaching English pronunciation.

BREAKING THE ICE

Teaching foreign accent reduction can and SHOULD be fun for all concerned. At first, students will invariably be apprehensive and self-conscious about taking such a course and "exposing" their speech patterns in front of you and their peers. The time you spend trying to alleviate their initial concerns will be time well spent. We recommend:

1. Using the first class meeting to discuss the positive aspects of "accents" in general. Elaborate on the information presented on page 2 in "To the Student."

2. Emphasizing that accent reduction is NOT the losing of one's culture or heritage, but the improvement of a skill, as is the ability to play the piano, guitar, or tennis! Our students relate well to such analogies.
3. Describing your own embarrassing mistakes or those of other native Americans when speaking a foreign language. Our students laugh heartily at our examples and are comforted by the thought that we, too, experience pronunciation difficulties when speaking our second language.

HEARING THE SOUNDS

Advise your students that their initial difficulty in hearing the various vowel sounds is perfectly normal. Non-native speakers of English frequently have difficulty recognizing sounds absent in their native language. (Scholes found that the sound system of one's native language will influence his or her perception of English phonemes.) Your students will overcome this initial "deafness" to specific sounds after directed auditory discrimination practice. If possible, ask your school nurse, speech pathologist, or local public health department to administer a quick, routine hearing screening to each of your students. This will dissolve their concerns (and yours!) about any possibility of hearing loss.

ACCENT ANALYSIS

The Accent Analysis should be used at the beginning of the **English Pronunciation for International Students** program. Record each student (or have them record themselves at home) reading the Accent Analysis Sentences—Consonants on page 258 and Accent Analysis Sentences—Vowels on page 265. Each pair is designed to survey the students' pronunciation of a specific target consonant or vowel. Encourage them to read the sentences in a natural, conversational voice. The Accent Analysis should be used again when your students complete the program. This will help you (and them) measure their progress.

Now you are ready to listen to your students' tapes and do a written survey of their pronunciation difficulties with consonants, vowels, diphthongs, and word stress. The Summary of Errors—Consonants form on page 263 and the Summary of Errors—Vowels on page 268 provide a place to record the results. The pairs of Accent Analysis Sentences are numbered to correspond with the phonetic symbols.

As each group of sentences is read, listen only to the pronunciation of the **target sound.** Ignore all other errors. While a student is reading, follow along sentence by sentence on the **Teacher's Record Form.** Circle all target words that are mispronounced. On the line above the mispronounced target word, record the error. Use any marking (e.g., phonetic) which is meaningful to you. You can then complete the **Summary of Errors Forms** at your leisure.

EXAMPLE: Your student substitutes [s] (as in *sit*) and [t] (as in *to*) for [θ] in sentence 5's target words *think, nothing,* and *threat, third,* respectively. You might record the errors as follows:

       _[t]_   __   _[t]_

5.   Is there a ***threat?*** of World War ***Three?*** After a ***third*** war, many

    _[s]_   _[s]_   __   ___

    think there will be ***nothing*** left on ***earth***. We must be ***thankful***

    for peace.

On the **Summary of Errors** form, you might note the following:

CONSONANTS	Correct	Error	Comments
5. [θ] as in *think*	_____	[s] & [t] for [θ]	*errors are inconsistent*

EXAMPLE: Your student substitutes [aʊ] (as in *out*) for [ɔ] in sentence 9's target words *author* and *audience,* and [oʊ] (as in *no*) in *office* and *boring.* You might record the errors as follows:

      _[aʊ]_   _   _   _[oʊ]_   __   _[aʊ]_

[ɔ]9. The ***author*** gave a ***long talk*** in the ***office.*** The ***small audience***

    ___   _[oʊ]_

    thought it was ***boring.***

On the **Summary of Errors** form, you might make the following notations:

VOWELS	Correct	Error	Comments
			Errors seem related to
9. [ɔ] as in *ALL*	_____	[aʊ] & [oʊ] for [ɔ]	*spelling patterns.*

ACCENT ANALYSIS SENTENCES: CONSONANTS

1. The United States started with 13 small states. Now there are 50 states spread from east to west.

2. Lazy cows graze in the fields of New Zealand. The pleasant breeze blows from the seas.

3. *A Tale of Two Cities* was written by Charles Dickens. Today it is taught throughout the world.

4. Dad had a bad cold. He stayed in bed all day Monday and Tuesday.

5. Is there a threat of World War Three? After a third war, many think there will be nothing left on earth. We must be thankful for peace.

6. My mother and father loathe northern weather. They prefer the climate of the southern states.

7. Sherry took a short vacation to Washington. She went fishing and found shells along the ocean shore.

8. Chuck ate lunch in the kitchen. He had a cheese sandwich and peach pie.

9. I made a decision to paint the garage beige. I usually paint or watch television in my leisure time.

10. George is majoring in education. He will graduate from college next June.

11. Year after year, millions of people visit New York. Young and old enjoy familiar sights.

12. Pick up a pack of ripe apples. Mom will bake apple pie for supper.

13. Bob built a big boat. He finds lobster and crab and cooks them in the cabin below.

14. The elephant is friendly and full of life. It's a fact that an elephant never forgets!

15. Leave the veal and gravy in the oven. Vicky wants to keep it very hot. She will serve everyone at seven.

16. Kathy can't bake for the card party. She is working at the bank until six o'clock.

17. Gambling is legal in Las Vegas. Gamblers go for the big win!

18. We would like to see the Seven Wonders of the World. We will just have to wait awhile!

19. Roads are rough in rural areas. Be very careful when you drive your car.

20. I like the cooler climate in the fall. The gold and yellow colors of the leaves are beautiful.

21. Heaven helps those who help themselves. Anyhow, hard work never hurt anyone.

22. I'm coming home for Christmas. As the poem says, "Wherever you may roam, there's no place like home."

23. Now you can learn to pronounce the consonants. Practice them again and again on your own.

24. The strong young men are exercising this morning. They are running long distances.

25. Mother washed, cooked, and cleaned. After she finished, she rested.

26. Put the shoes and boots in the boxes. Hang the dresses and pants on the hangers.

Teacher's Record Form

[s] 1. The United **States started** with 13 **small states.** Now there are 50 **states spread** from **east** to **west.**

[z] 2. **Lazy cows graze** in the **fields** of New **Zealand.** The **pleasant breeze blows** from the **seas.**

[t] 3. A **Tale** of **Two Cities** was **written** by Charles Dickens. **Today it** is **taught throughout** the world.

[d] 4. **Dad had a bad cold.** He **stayed** in **bed** all **day Monday and Tuesday.**

[θ] 5. Is there a **threat** of World War **Three?** After a **third** war, many **think** there will be **nothing** left on **earth.** We must be **thankful** for peace.

[ð] 6. My **mother** and **father loathe northern weather. They** prefer **the** climate of **the southern** states.

[ʃ] 7. **Sherry** took a **short vacation** to **Washington. She** went **fishing** and found **shells** along the **ocean shore.**

[tʃ] 8. **Chuck** ate **lunch** in the **kitchen.** He had a **cheese sandwich** and **peach** pie.

[ʒ] 9. I made a **decision** to paint the **garage beige.** I **usually** paint or watch **television** in my **leisure** time.

[dʒ] 10. **Georgē** is **mājoring** in **ēducation.** He will **graduate** from

collēge next **June.**

[j] 11. **Yēar** after **yēar, millions** of people visit New **York. Young**

and old enjoy **familiar** sights.

[p] 12. **Pick up** a **pack** of **ripe apples.** Mom will bake **apple pie**

for **supper.**

[b] 13. **Bob built** a **big boat.** He finds **lobster** and **crab** and cooks

them in the **cabin below.**

[f] 14. The **elephant** is **friendly** and **full** of **life.** It's a **fact** that an

elephant never **forgets!**

[v] 15. **Lēave** the **vēal** and **grāvy** in the **ōven. Vicky** wants to keep

it **vēry** hot. She will **serve everyone** at **sēven.**

[k] 16. **Kathy can't bāke** a **cake** for the **card** party. She is **working**

at the **bank** until six **o'clock.**

[g] 17. **Gambling** is **lēgal** in Las **Vegas. Gamblers go** for the **big** win!

[w] 18. **Wē would** like to see the Seven **Wonders** of the **World. Wē**

will just have to **wait awhile!**

[r] 19. **Rōads āre rough** in **rural āreas.** Be **very careful** when

you **drive your car.**

[l] 20. I **līke** the **cooler climate** in the **fall.** The **gold** and **yellow**

colors of the **leaves** are **beautiful.**

[h]   21. **Heaven helps** those **who help** themselves. **Anyhow, hard** work never **hurt** anyone.

[m]   22. **I'm coming home** for **Christmas.** As the **poem** says, "Wherever you **may roam,** there's no place like **home.**"

[n]   23. **Now** you **can learn** to **pronounce** the **consonants.** Practice them **again and again on** your **own.**

[ŋ]   24. The **strong young** men are **exercising** this **morning.** They are **running long** distances.

PAST TENSE

25.   Mother wash**ed**, cook**ed**, and clean**ed**. After she finish**ed**, she rest**ed**.

PLURALS

26.   Put the shoe**s** and boot**s** in the box**es.** Hang the dress**es** and pant**s** on the hanger**s.**

Student's Name: _____ Date: _____

SUMMARY OF ERRORS: CONSONANTS

CONSONANTS	CORRECT	ERROR		COMMENTS
1. [s] as in *see*	_____	_____	for [s]	_____
2. [z] as in *zoo*	_____	_____	for [z]	_____
3. [t] as in *too*	_____	_____	for [t]	_____
4. [d] as in *dog*	_____	_____	for [d]	_____
5. [θ] as in *think*	_____	_____	for [θ]	_____
6. [ð] as in *them*	_____	_____	for [ð]	_____
7. [ʃ] as in *shoe*	_____	_____	for [ʃ]	_____
8. [tʃ] as in *chair*	_____	_____	for [tʃ]	_____
9. [ʒ] as in *rouge*	_____	_____	for [ʒ]	_____
10. [dʒ] as in *jaw*	_____	_____	for [dʒ]	_____
11. [j] as in *you*	_____	_____	for [j]	_____
12. [p] as in *pay*	_____	_____	for [p]	_____
13. [b] as in *boy*	_____	_____	for [b]	_____
14. [f] as in *foot*	_____	_____	for [f]	_____
15. [v] as in *very*	_____	_____	for [v]	_____
16. [k] as in *key*	_____	_____	for [k]	_____
17. [g] as in *go*	_____	_____	for [g]	_____
18. [w] as in *we*	_____	_____	for [w]	_____
19. [r] as in *red*	_____	_____	for [r]	_____
20. [l] as in *look*	_____	_____	for [l]	_____
21. [h] as in *hat*	_____	_____	for [h]	_____
22. [m] as in *me*	_____	_____	for [m]	_____
23. [n] as in *no*	_____	_____	for [n]	_____
24. [ŋ] as in *ring*	_____	_____	for [ŋ]	_____

PAST TENSE

	CORRECT	INCORRECT	COMMENTS
a. [t] as in wash*ed*			
b. [d] as in clean*ed*			
c. [ɪd] as in rest*ed*			

PLURALS

a. [z] as in shoe*s*			
b. [s] as in boot*s*			
c. [ɪz] as in dress*es*			

ARE FINAL CONSONANTS CLEAR?

OTHER OBSERVATIONS:

ACCENT ANALYSIS SENTENCES: VOWELS

1. Please believe that sweet peas and beans are good to eat. Eat them at least twice a week.

2. Tim's sister swims a little bit. It keeps her fit, slim, and trim.

3. Ten times seven is seventy. Seven times eleven is seventy-seven.

4. Many animals inhabit Africa. Africa has camels, giraffes, parrots, and bats.

5. Doctors say jogging is good for the body. Lots of starch causes heart problems.

6. Who flew to the moon? Numerous lunar flights are in the news. We'll soon put a man on Jupiter and Pluto.

7. Would you look for my cookbook? It should be full of hints for good cookies and pudding.

8. The southern governor is Republican. The public election was fun. He won by one hundred votes.

9. The author gave a long talk in the office. The small audience thought it was boring.

10. Nurses do worthy work. They certainly deserve a word of praise.

11. Labor Day is in September. Workers are honored.

12. Maine is a state in the northern United States. It's a great place for a vacation.

13. The North Pole is close to the Arctic Ocean. It's known for polar bears, snow, and severe cold.

14. Owls are now found throughout the world. They avoid crowds and make loud sounds.

15. Eyesight is vital for a normal life. I prize mine highly.

16. The auto industry is a loyal employer in Detroit. People enjoy their choice of cars.

17. Africa, Asia, Australia, South America, and Europe comprise five of the continents. North America is the other continent.

18. I have televisions in the bedroom, living room, and dining room. The programs about detectives and hospitals are my favorite.

Teachers's Record Form

[i]   1. **Please believe** that **sweet peas** and **beans** are good to **eat**. **Eat** them at **least** twice a **week**.

[ɪ]   2. **Tim's sister swims** a **little bit**. **It** keeps her **fit, slim** and **trim**.

[ɛ]   3. **Ten** times **seven** is **seventy**. **Seven** times **eleven** is **seventy-seven**.

[æ]   4. Many **animals inhabit Africa**. **Africa has camels, giraffes, parrots,** and **bats**.

[a]   5. **Doctors** say **jogging** is good for the **body**. **Lots** of **starch** causes **heart problems**.

[u]   6. **Who flew to** the **moon? Numerous lunar** flights are in the **news**. We'll **soon** put a man on **Jupiter** and **Pluto**.

[ʊ]   7. **Would** you **look** for my **cookbook?** It **should** be **full** of hints for **good cookies** and **pudding**.

[ʌ]   8. The **southern governor** is **Republican**. The **public** election **was fun**. He **won** by **one hundred** votes.

[ɔ]   9. The **author** gave a **long talk** in the **office**. The **small audience thought** it was **boring**.

[ɝ]   10. **Nurses** do **worthy work**. They **certainly deserve** a **word** of praise.

[ɚ]   11. **La**bor Day is in **September. Workers** are **honored.**

[eɪ]   12. **Maine** is a **state** in the northern United **States.** It's a **great place** for a **vacation.**

[oʊ]   13. The North **Pole** is **close** to the Arctic **Ocean.** It's **known** for **polar** bears, **snow,** and severe **cold.**

[aʊ]   14. **Owls** are **now found throughout** the world. They avoid **crowds** and make **loud sounds.**

[aɪ]   15. **Eyesight** is **vital** for a normal **life. I prize mine highly.**

[ɔɪ]   16. The auto industry is a **loyal employer** in **Detroit.** People **enjoy** their **choice** of cars.

WORD STRESS

[ə]   17. **Africa, Asia, Australia,** South **America,** and **Europe** com-**prise five** of the **continents.** North **America** is the other **con**-**tinent.**

     18. I have **tele**visions in the **bed**room, **living** room, and **dining** room. The **pro**grams a**bout** de**tec**tives and **hos**pitals are my **fav**orites.*

*The boldface letters indicate the syllable that should receive primary stress. If the student errs on a target word, circle the incorrectly stressed syllable.

Student's Name_____

Date: _____

SUMMARY OF ERRORS: VOWELS

VOWELS	CORRECT	ERROR		COMMENTS
1. [i] as in *ME*	_____	_____	for [i]	_____
2. [ɪ] as in *IT*	_____	_____	for [ɪ]	_____
3. [ɛ] as in *EGG*	_____	_____	for [ɛ]	_____
4. [æ] as in *AT*	_____	_____	for [æ]	_____
5. [a] as in *HOT*	_____	_____	for [a]	_____
6. [u] as in *YOU*	_____	_____	for [u]	_____
7. [ʊ] as in *COOK*	_____	_____	for [ʊ]	_____
8. [ʌ] as in *UP*	_____	_____	for [ʌ]	_____
9. [ɔ] as in *ALL*	_____	_____	for [ɔ]	_____
10. [ɝ] as in *FIRST*	_____	_____	for [ɝ]	_____
11. [ɚ] as in *FATHER*	_____	_____	for [ɚ]	_____

DIPHTHONGS

	CORRECT	ERROR		COMMENTS
12. [eɪ] as in *ATE*	_____	_____	for [eɪ]	_____
13. [oʊ] as in *NO*	_____	_____	for [oʊ]	_____
14. [aʊ] as in *OUT*	_____	_____	for [aʊ]	_____
15. [aɪ] as in *MY*	_____	_____	for [aɪ]	_____
16. [ɔɪ] as in *BOY*	_____	_____	for [ɔɪ]	_____

WORD STRESS   CORRECT   INCORRECT   (Does not reduce in unstressed syllables)

17. [ə] as in *SODA*   _____   _____

18. Is stress placed on the wrong syllable of words of more than one syllable?

Errors:_____

OTHER OBSERVATIONS:

USING THE MANUAL FOR CLASSROOM INSTRUCTION

Whether you are an instructor of ESL, speech, or accent reduction, or a speech pathologist, you will find **English Pronunciation for International Students** completely adaptable for classroom or clinical use. The exercises and self-tests in the manual have been tested in the classroom and have proven to be effective with non-native speakers of English striving to improve their American English pronunciation. The manual is so complete that it eliminates the need for you to spend endless hours preparing drill materials. The following are some suggestions to help you use the manual effectively.

To the Student

Read this section first to familiarize yourself with the organization and content of the manual.

Sequence of Material Presentation

The order of sound presentation is flexible. The integrity of the program will remain intact if you assign the chapters in a sequence of your own choosing. Your personal teaching philosophy, available time, and students' specific needs should dictate what you teach first. Many students will not have difficulty with all the sounds. Consequently, you may wish to skip some chapters completely and spend more time on the *"real trouble-makers"* (like [ɪ] as in "it" or [ʊ] as in "cook")!

A Key to Pronouncing the Consonants and Vowels of American English

These sections introduce the International Phonetic Alphabet. Don't be concerned if you are currently unfamiliar with the phonetic symbols. Each symbol is introduced and explained one at a time. You will learn them easily and gradually as you progress through the program with your students. Refer back to the **Key to Pronouncing the Consonants of American English** (p.7) and the **Key to Pronouncing the Vowels of American English** (p.139) when you need to refresh your memory.

Adaptation of Material

The material presented in each chapter can be adapted easily. If your students require more drill at the sentence level before progressing to dialogues or paragraphs, focus your attention on the appropriate exercises; defer presentation of more difficult activities to a later time.

Self-Tests

The self-tests can be used in a variety of ways: (1) You can present the tests as described in the manual to evaluate your students' progress; (2) you can use them as both **PRE** and **POST** tests to more precisely measure students' gains; (3) you might prefer to divide your students into "teams" to complete the tests as a group rather than individually; or (4) you can assign the self-tests as homework to encourage out-of-class practice.

FOR AN ENCORE . . . .

The activities in this section can easily be expanded for classroom use. The diversity of these assignments will certainly liven up the regular classroom routine. For example, in the **[i]** and **[ɪ]** chapter, the students are asked to make several social introductions using phrases pronounced with the target sounds. This activity could be employed in the classroom by having students introduce themselves to each other.

SUPPLEMENTARY ACTIVITIES

As an extra bonus, here are some additional in-class activities to vary your presentation of the material in the manual.

Objective: To increase the student's ability to recognize the target sound auditorily.

    Activity 1: Read Exercise A words orally in mixed order. Have the students identify the target sound as occurring in either the initial, medial, or final position.

    Activity 2: Read phrase and sentence exercises orally. Have the students list all the words containing the target sound.

Objective: To increase the student's ability to discriminate between the target sound and his or her error.

    Activity 1: Use minimal pairs exercises/self-tests (e.g., Oral Exercise on page 150). Create word pairs such as **bit-bit** and **bit-beat.** Have the students identify the words in each pair as being the SAME or DIFFERENT.

Activity 2: Read orally from the minimal pairs exercises. Vary the order of the words (**bit–beat, seat–sit**). Have the students indicate whether they heard the target vowel in the first or second word.

Activity 3: Give a "spelling test." Read individual words from the minimal pairs exercises. Have your students write the words as you say them. This is a sure way to determine if they are hearing the target sound.

Activity 4: Read the phrase and sentence exercises orally. Alternate between imitating a student's typical error and pronouncing the target sound correctly. Have your students determine whether or not the words in the phrases and sentences have been produced accurately.

Objective: To increase the student's ability to produce the target sound.

Activity 1: Have your students role-play using the self-test dialogues at the end of each chapter.

> Example for target consonant [v]: "I'm going on ***vacation*** and ***I've*** packed a ***vest, vase, stove . . .***"

Objective: To increase the students' ability to correctly pronounce past tense and plural endings.

Activity 1: Play a question-and-answer game using regular present and past tense verbs. Ask one student to respond in a complete sentence to your question; then ask a yes or no question of another student. The next student must respond to the question, pronouncing the verb correctly in the past tense, and ask a question of his own.

> Example: "When did you stop smoking?" "I **stopped** smoking last year!" "Did you wash your car today?" "No, I **washed** it yesterday."

Activity 2: Present a variety of three-verb series aloud. (One past tense verb in each series should have a different **ed** sound than the other two.) Ask the students to identify the verb with the different **ed** sound.

> Example: You say **baked**, **cleaned**, **cooked**; the students should select **cleaned**.

Activity 3: Play a "bragging" game using various noun categories.

> Example: One student says, "*I have two **cars**! How*
> $\qquad\qquad\qquad\qquad\qquad\qquad\qquad$ [z]

> *many **cars** do you have?" "I have three **cars**! and*
> $\quad$ [z] $\qquad\qquad\qquad\qquad\qquad\qquad$ [z]

> *two **boats**"; or "I ate four **eggs** and two **pieces***
> $\quad$ [s] $\qquad\qquad\qquad\qquad$ [z] $\qquad\qquad$ [ɪz]
> *of bacon. What did you eat?" etc.*

With all these suggestions and the activities described in the manual, your students will be kept occupied and learning throughout the course!

APPENDIX II
ANSWERS

ANSWERS TO SELF-TEST I ON PAGE 14

1. 1   2   (rice   lice)
2. 1   ②   (lake   rake)
3. ①   2   (belly   berry)
4. ①   2   (rent   lent)
5. 1   ②   (lime   rhyme)
   ○

ANSWERS TO SELF-TEST I ON PAGE 17

1. read   bread / tread
2. right   bright / fright
3. rip   drip / trip
4. ream   dream / cream
5. row   crow / grow
6. rain   brain / train / grain
7. rash   brash / crash / trash
8. room   broom / groom —
9. round   ground
10. race   brace / grace / trace

ANSWERS TO REVIEW TEST I ON PAGE 20

1. 1   2   3   (lied   lied   ride)   6. 1   2   3   (collect   correct   correct)
2. 1   2   ③   (low   row   low)   7. ①   2   3   (long   wrong   long)
3. 1   ②   3   (crew   crew   clue)   8. 1   ②   3   (arrive   arrive   alive)
4. 1   2   ③   (late   rate   rate)   9. 1   2   ③   (race   lace   race)
5. ①   2   3   (glass   glass   grass)   10. 1   ②   3   (clue   crew   crew)
        ○   ○

ANSWERS TO REVIEW TEST II ON PAGE 21

1. Don't step on the   (glass   (grass).
                                [l]   [r]

2. Please put this on your   (list   wrist).
                                  [l]   [r]

3. The whole family was   (pleasant   present).
                                  [l]   [r]

4. It was a horrid   (climb   (crime).
                                  [l]   [r]

5. Look at the bright red   (flame   (frame).
                                  [l]   [r]

ANSWERS TO REVIEW TEST III ON PAGE 22

1.   read   (Did you <u>lead</u> the book?)

2.   bloom   (The flowers are in <u>broom</u>.)

3.   lake   (Take a swim in the <u>rake</u>.)

4.   lock   (Be sure to <u>rock</u> the door.)

5.   correct   (The answer was <u>collect</u>.)

ANSWERS TO SELF-TEST I ON PAGE 25

1. shin   C   (I)
2. ship   C   (I)
3. simmer   (C)   I
4. single   (C)   I
5. she's   C   (I)

ANSWERS FOR SELF-TEST I ON PAGE 30

1. s u p p o (s) e
2. S u (s) a n
3. d i (s) a s t e r
4. e a (s) i e s t
5. t i s s u e (s)

ANSWERS TO SELF-TEST I ON PAGE 33

1. (two (too)) Tess had _____ much to eat.
2. ((two) too) I must return _____ TVs.
3. ((right) write) "Two wrongs don't make a _____."
4. (right (write)) Please _____ me a note.
5. ((aunt) ant) Tim's _____ is twenty-two.

ANSWERS TO SELF-TEST II ON PAGE 33

TIM: (Tina), who were you (talking) (to) on the (telephone)?

TINA: (Terry) (White). She (wanted) (to) know (what) (time) the (party) is (tonight).

TIM: (Terry) is always (late). She (missed)* our (tennis) game (last) (Tuesday).

TINA: (Two) days ago, she (didn't) come (to) (breakfast) (until) (two). (Terry) is always in a (tizzy)!

TIM: (Terry) (missed) her (flight) (to) (Tucson) (last) week.

TINA: (That) (routine) of hers is (typical)!

TIM: This is (terrible)! (What) (time) did you (tell) her (to) come (tonight)?

TINA: I (told) (Terry) (to) come (at) six (fifteen). The (party) is really (at) (eight)!

TIM: (To) (tell) the (truth), I wish you (told) her (it) was (at) (two). I (don't) (trust) her!

ANSWERS TO SELF-TEST I ON PAGE 37

Mr. (and) Mrs. (Ed) (Dean)
cordially invite you
to the (wedding) of their (daughter)
(WENDY) (DEAN)
to
(DAN) (DEWEY)
on (Sunday), the twenty-(third) of (December),
at the (Diner's) Club
1020 (Davis) (Road), (Dodge), North (Dakota)

RECEPTION (AND) (DINNER) FOLLOWING (WEDDING)

RSVP by (Wednesday), (December) (third)

---

*The letters -ed in "missed" sound like [t]. (Refer to p. 126 Pronouncing Past Tense Verbs.)

ANSWERS TO SELF-TEST I ON PAGE 41

Do you know (anything) about Jim (Thorpe?) He was an American Indian (athlete.) He excelled in (everything) at the Olympics. (Thousands) were angry when (Thorpe's) medals were taken away because he was called a professional (athlete.) In (1973,) long after his (death,) (Thorpe)'s medals were restored. (Throughout) the world, Jim (Thorpe) is (thought) to be one of the greatest male (athletes.)

ANSWERS TO SELF-TEST I ON PAGE 46

(The) Photo Album

DAUGHTER:	(Mother,) I like (these) old pictures. Who's (this?)
MOTHER:	(That's) your great (grandmother.)
DAUGHTER:	(The) (feathered) hat is funny! Who's (that) man?
MOTHER:	(That's) your (grandfather.) He was from (the) (Netherlands.)
DAUGHTER:	I know (these) people! Aren't (they) Uncle Tom and Uncle Bob?
MOTHER:	(That's) right. (Those) are my (brothers). (They) always (bothered) me!
DAUGHTER:	(This) must be (either) (father) or his (brother.)
MOTHER:	(Neither)! (That's) your (father's) uncle.
DAUGHTER:	Why are (there) (other) people in (this) photo?
MOTHER:	(This) was a family (gathering.) We got (together) all (the) time.
DAUGHTER:	(Mother), who's (this) "(smooth)"-looking man?
MOTHER:	Shhhhhhhhh! I'd (rather) not say. Your (father) will hear!
DAUGHTER:	Is (that) your old boyfriend?
MOTHER:	Well, even (mothers) had fun in (those) days!

ANSWERS TO SELF-TEST I ON PAGE 49

1.	crush	cash	(catch)	crash
2.	chef	(chief)	chute	chiffon
3.	machine	parachute	mustache	(kitchen)
4.	(China)	Russia	Chicago	Michigan
5.	musician	physician	(chemist)	electrician
6.	pressure	(pressed)	assure	permission
7.	(division)	subtraction	addition	multiplication
8.	position	action	(patio)	motion
9.	Charlotte	Cheryl	Sharon	(Charles)
10.	tension	(resign)	pension	mention

ANSWERS TO SELF-TEST I ON PAGE 53

1. The **commission** made a **decision**.
   [ʃ]   [ʒ]

2. The class learned **division** and **addition**.
          [ʒ]   [ʃ]

3. **Measure** the **garage**.
      [ʒ]   [ʒ]

4. Your **profession** has **prestige**.
        [ʃ]   [ʒ]

5. That's an **unusual shade** of **rouge**.
          [ʒ] [ʃ]   [ʒ]

ANSWERS TO SELF-TEST I ON PAGE 57

1. Ⓒ   I   (The dress was **cheap**.)
2. C   Ⓘ   (Always **shoe** your food.)
3. C   Ⓘ   (I ate a **tease** sandwich.)
4. C   Ⓘ   (My **wash** keeps perfect time.)
5. Ⓒ   I   (**March** is a windy month.)

ANSWERS TO SELF-TEST I ON PAGE 61

(Java)	Guatemala	(Jerusalem)	Greece
England	(Germany)	(Jamaica)	Hungary
(Japan)	Greenland	(Algeria)	(Egypt)
(Belgium)	(Argentina)	China	Luxembourg

ANSWERS TO SELF-TEST I ON PAGE 64

1. The **youth** left. He hasn't come back **YET**.
2. The player ran 50 **yards**. The crowds began to **YELL**.
3. Today is Monday. **YESTERDAY** was Sunday.
4. Egg **yolks** should be **YELLOW**.
5. **You** should get a checkup once a **YEAR**.

ANSWERS TO SELF-TEST II ON PAGE 65

1. (SAME) DIFFERENT (I had to **yawn**. I had to **yawn**.)
2. SAME (DIFFERENT) (Did you say **yolk**? Did you say **oak**?)
3. SAME (DIFFERENT) (It's not **yellow**. It's not **jello**.)
4. (SAME) DIFFERENT (They left **yesterday**. They left **yesterday**.)
5. SAME (DIFFERENT) (Find the **major**. Find the **mayor**.)

ANSWERS TO REVIEW TEST I ON PAGE 69

   [θ] [z]
1. thou<u>s</u>an<u>d</u>

   [s] [θ] [s]
2. <u>s</u>ou<u>th</u>we<u>s</u>t

   [ð] [z]
3. <u>th</u>e<u>s</u>e

    [θ] [t]
4. a<u>thl</u>ete

     [θ]   [d]
5. bir<u>th</u>day car<u>d</u>

ANSWERS TO REVIEW TEST II ON PAGE 70

<u>2</u>	<u>3</u>	<u>1</u>
1. ear	jeer	year
<u>3</u>	<u>2</u>	<u>1</u>
2. cheap	jeep	sheep
<u>1</u>	<u>3</u>	<u>2</u>
3. sue	shoe	zoo
<u>1</u>	<u>2</u>	<u>3</u>
4. cello	jello	yellow
<u>2</u>	<u>1</u>	<u>3</u>
5. tease	cheese	she's

ANSWERS TO REVIEW TEST III ON PAGE 71

1. Did you make the (**bed** / bet)?
            [d]   [t]

2. We need a second (**seat** / sheet).
            [s]   [ʃ]

3. Count up your (chips / **tips**).
            [tʃ]   [t]

4. I like to (**raise** / race) horses.
           [z]   [s]

5. Matthew took the (**bath** / bat).
            [θ]   [t]

6. (Teasing / **Teething**) makes the baby cry.
   [z]   [ð]

7. Before you know it, (they / **Jay**) will be here.
               [ð] [dʒ]

8. Her words were spoken with (zest / **jest**).
                 [z] [dʒ]

ANSWERS TO REVIEW TEST IV ON PAGE 72

1. __5__ [j]
   onion
   union
   million
   billion

2. __1__ [ʃ]
   chef
   chute
   chic
   chiffon

3. __2__ [tʃ]
   nature
   picture
   capture
   furniture

4. __3__ [ʒ]
   division
   occasion
   explosion
   television

5. __1__ [ʃ]
   Russia
   tissue
   passion
   mission

6. __4__ [dʒ]
   gradual
   cordial
   soldier
   education

7. __2__ [tʃ]
   chief
   catch
   question
   ketchup

8. __6__ [z]
   rose
   xerox
   eyes
   cousin
   sneeze

9. __5__ [j]
   cute
   yawn
   amuse
   senior

10. __4__ [dʒ]
    ridge
    angel
    suggest
    general

11. __3__ [ʒ]
    vision
    rouge
    garage
    pleasure

12. __6__ [z]
    season
    bugs
    husband
    zone
    maze

ANSWERS TO SELF-TEST I ON PAGE 75

The (Surprise) (Trip)

PETE: (Paulette), I have a (surprise)! We're taking a (trip) tonight!

PAULETTE: I'm very (happy). But I need more time to (prepare).

PETE: That's (simple). I'll (help) you (pack).

PAULETTE: Who will care for our (pet) (poodle)?

PETE: Your (parents)!

PAULETTE: Who will (pick) (up) the mail?

PETE: Our neighbor (Pat).

PAULETTE: Who will water the (plants)?

PETE: We'll (put) them on the (patio).

PAULETTE: Who will (pay) for the (trip)?

PETE: The (company) is (paying) every (penny)!

PAULETTE: (Pete), you've really (planned) this.

PETE: Of course! I'm (dependable), (superior), and a (perfect). . .

PAULETTE: "(Pain) in the neck!"* Don't get carried away!

ANSWERS TO SELF-TEST I ON PAGE 78

BETTY: (Ben), I (bet) you forgot my (birthday)!

BEN: I (bet) I didn't. I (bought) you a (birthday) present.

BETTY: I can't (believe) it. What did you (bring)?

BEN: It (begins) with the letter (**B**).

BETTY: Oh, (boy)! It must be a (bathrobe). You (buy) me one every (birthday).

BEN: It's not a (bathrobe)!

BETTY: Is it a (bowling) (ball)?

BEN: No, it's not a (bowling) (ball).

BETTY: It must (be) a (book) (about) (boating) your favorite (hobby).

BEN: (Betty), you're way off (base). I (bought) you a (bracelet). A diamond (bracelet)!

BETTY: Wow! This is the (best) (birthday) present I ever got. You didn't (rob) a (bank), did you?

BEN: Don't worry. I didn't (beg), (borrow), or steal; just don't expect any more presents for a long time. I'm (broke)!

ANSWERS TO SELF-TEST I ON PAGE 83

1. **Find** another name **for** a drugstore.   pharmacy
2. **Find** another name **for** a doctor.   physician
3. **Find** another name **for** a snapshot.   photograph
4. **Find** the name **for** a person who studies **philosophy**.   philosopher
5. **Find** the short **form** of the word *telephone*.   phone
6. **Find** another name **for** a record player.   phonograph
7. **Find** the name **for** a person who predicts the **future**.   prophet
8. **Find** the name **for** the study of sounds.   phonetics
9. **Find** the term that **refers** to your sister's son.   nephew
10. **Find** the name for a chart showing **figures**.   graph

ANSWERS TO SELF-TEST II ON PAGE 83

(Florida) was (founded) by Ponce de Leon in (15)13. This (famous) explorer (from) Spain was searching (for) a (fountain) of youth. He named the land (Florida), which means "(full) of (flowers)" in Spanish. He (failed) in his (efforts) to (find) the (fountain). He (finally) died (after) (fighting) the Indians. (Unfortunately), no one has ever (found) the (fountain) in (Florida) or the (formula) (for) eternal youth. However, the (fun) and sun in (Florida) are (enough) to attract (folks) (from) every (hemisphere) to this (famous) American state.

ANSWERS TO SELF-TEST I ON PAGE 87

1. B   M   (E)   (have)
2. B   (M)   E   (heavy)
3. (B)   M   E   (very)
4. (B)   M   E   (victory)
5. B   (M)   E   (oven)

ANSWERS TO SELF-TEST II ON PAGE 88

I (Never) Saw a Moor

I (never) saw a moor,
I (never) saw the sea;
Yet know I how the heather looks,
And what a (wave) must be.

I (never) spoke with God,
Nor (visited) in (Heaven);
Yet certain am I (of) the spot
As if the chart were (given).

ANSWERS TO SELF-TEST I ON PAGE 91

(Ohio)   Michigan   (Oklahoma)   (Houston)
(Idaho)   Massachusetts   Washington   (New Hampshire)
Chicago   (Hartford)   (Hawaii)   (Tallahassee)

ANSWERS TO SELF-TEST II ON PAGE 92

HELEN: (Hi) Mom. Welcome (home). (How) was (Hawaii)?
MOTHER: Like a second (honeymoon)! I'm as (happy) as a lark. (How) are you?
HELEN: (Horrible)! (Henry) is in the (hospital) with a broken (hip).
MOTHER: (How) did that (happen)?
HELEN: He (heard) a noise outside. (He) went (behind) the (house) and fell over a (hose).
MOTHER: (How) are my (handsome) grandsons?
HELEN: They won't (behave). And my (housekeeper) (had) to quit.
MOTHER: (Perhaps) you'd like me to (help) at (home).
HELEN: Oh, Mom, I was (hoping) you'd say that. (Hurry) to the (house) as soon as possible.
MOTHER: I guess the (honeymoon) is over. (Here) we go again!

ANSWERS TO SELF-TEST I ON PAGE 95

(Woodrow) (Wilson)

(Woodrow) (Wilson) (was) the (twenty)-fifth president of the United States. He (will) (always) be remembered for his (work) to establish (world) peace. (Wilson) (was) born in 1865 and later (went) to Princeton University. He became president in 1913 and stayed in the (White) House for two terms. His first (wife) died (while) he (was) in office, and he married a (Washington) (widow). When the United States entered (World) (War) (I) in 1917, (Wilson) (quickly) provided the needed (wisdom). After the (war), (Wilson) made a (nationwide) tour to (win) support for the League of Nations. (Wilson) (was) (awarded) the Nobel Prize for his (worthwhile) (work) for peace. He died in (1924). (Everywhere) in the (world), (Wilson) (was) thought of as a (wise) and (wonderful) leader.

ANSWERS TO SELF-TEST II ON PAGE 96

1. **When was Woodrow Wilson** born?
   Woodrow Wilson was born in _____1865_____.
2. How many **wives** did **Wilson** have **while** in the **White** House?
   Wilson had _____two_____ **wives.**
3. **When** did the United States enter **World War I?**
   The United States entered **World War I** in _____1917_____.
4. **Why was Wilson awarded** the Nobel Prize?
   Wilson was awarded the Nobel Prize for his _worthwhile work for peace_.
5. **Where was Wilson** thought of as a **wise** and **wonderful** leader?
   Wilson was thought of as a **wise** and **wonderful** leader _everywhere in the world_.

ANSWERS TO REVIEW TEST I ON PAGE 98

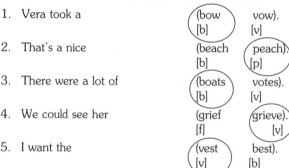

1. Vera took a — (bow [b] / vow [v]).
2. That's a nice — (beach [b] / (peach) [p]).
3. There were a lot of — (boats [b] / votes [v]).
4. We could see her — (grief [f] / (grieve) [v]).
5. I want the — ((vest) [v] / best [b]).

ANSWERS TO REVIEW TEST II ON PAGE 99

1. ____cab____ (The **cap** took us home.)
2. ____vase____ (Put the flowers in a **phase.**)
3. ____wine____ (White **vine** should be cold.)
4. ____leave____ (Don't **leaf** so early.)
5. ____laugh____ (The joke made him **lap.**)

ANSWERS TO REVIEW TEST III ON PAGES 99–100

[p]	[b]	[f]
Aesop's	fable	definition
people	valuable	fable
grapes	brief	brief
jumping	above	faults
up	but	fox
probably	became	fine
	probably	from
		finally
		famous
		left

[v]	[h]	[w]
of	his	well
valuable	hungry	once
very	he	was
virtues	hanging	want
above		
vine		
gave		

ANSWERS TO SELF-TEST I ON PAGE 103

The (American) (Cowboy)

(Americans) (created) the name (cowboy) for the men who (cared) for the (cattle.) You
might (recall) the (typical) singing (cowboy) in the movies. He was (kind,) (courageous,) and
good (looking.) He always (caught) the (cow,) (colt,) and of (course,) the girl! But the real
(cowboy) was a hard (worker) who had many (difficult) (tasks.) He had to (take) the (cattle) to
(market.) These lonely (cattle) drives (took) many (weeks) through rough (country.) The
(cowboy) had to (protect) the (cattle) and (keep) them from running off. In (fact) or (fiction,)
the (cowboy) will (continue) to be a (likeable) (American) (character.) **Ride 'em (cowboy!)**

ANSWERS TO SELF-TEST I ON PAGE 106

1. lag   (lack)
2. (bug)   buck
3. (league)   leak
4. (peg)   peck
5. nag   (knack)

ANSWERS TO SELF-TEST II ON PAGE 107

BREAKFAST

(Grapefruit)   (Eggs)   (Yogurt)   Sausage

LUNCH

(Hamburgers)   (Grilled Onions)   Gelatin   (Vinegar Dressing)

COCKTAILS

(Margarita)   Gin and Tonic   (Burgundy Wine)   (Grand Marnier)

DINNER

Lasagna   (Leg of Lamb)   (Green Peas)   (Gumbo)

DESSERT

Angel Food Cake   (Sugar Cookies)   (Grapes)   (Figs)

ANSWERS TO SELF-TEST I ON PAGE 110

1. ① 2   (clam   clan)
2. 1 ②   (tin   Tim)
3. ① 2   (bam   ban)
4. ① 2   (rum   run)
5. 1 ②   (sung   sum)

ANSWERS TO SELF-TEST I ON PAGE 113

1. S Ⓓ   (It's the **sane** thing. It's the **same** thing.)
2. Ⓢ D   (Pick up the **phone**. Pick up the **phone**.)
3. S Ⓓ   (He is my **kin**. He is my **king**.)
4. Ⓢ D   (This is **fun**. This is **fun**.)
5. S Ⓓ   (Please don't **sin**. Please don't **sing**.)

ANSWERS TO SELF-TEST I ON PAGE 116

1. (bring)   6. tangerine   11. (along)   16. engage
2. (anger)   7. (swing)   12. (talking)   17. (stinging)
3. (hang)   8. (tangle)   13. sponge   18. stingy
4. angel   9. danger   14. grin   19. lunch
5. (dancing)   10. (sink)   15. (running)   20. (bank)

ANSWERS TO REVIEW TEST I ON PAGE 118

1. Jean sat in the _____   (sum   (sun)   sung)
2. The bird hurt its _____   (whim   win   (wing))
3. It is fun to _____   (rum   (run)   rung)
4. The meat needs to_____   (simmer)   sinner   singer)
5. They removed the_____   (bam   (ban)   or   (band))

ANSWERS TO REVIEW TEST II ON PAGE 118

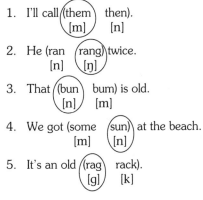

1. I'll call ((them) then).
          [m]   [n]

2. He (ran (rang) twice.
      [n]   [ŋ]

3. That ((bun) bum) is old.
         [n]   [m]

4. We got (some (sun) at the beach.
             [m]   [n]

5. It's an old ((rag) rack).
               [g]   [k]

ANSWERS TO REVIEW TEST III ON PAGE 119

ANNOUNCER:
                         [n]   [ŋ]   [ŋ] [n]   [ŋ]
Is your ski**n** feeli**ng** dry? Are you findi**ng** **n**ew wri**n**kles,

        [g]   [n]   [n]   [m] [n]   [m]
ba**g**s, and li**n**es? The**n** you need Po**m**'s Ski**n** Crea**m**. Men

          [n]   [g]   [n]
and wome**n** everywhere bra**g** about our cream. Liste**n** to

         [m]   [m]   [n]   [ŋ]
famous fil**m** star **M**olly Malo**n**e who has been acti**ng** for a

  [ŋ]   [ŋ]   [ŋ]
lo**ng**, lo**ng**, lo**ng** time.

MOLLY:
                                  [n] [n]
Hmmmmmm. Of course, everyo**n**e **kn**ows I started mak-

  [ŋ]   [m]   [n]   [n]   [ŋ]
i**ng** fil**m**s whe**n** I was ni**n**e. But I've been usi**ng** Pom's

               [ŋ]   [n]
Cream for years and I thi**nk** it's wo**n**derful. Just put it on

      [ŋ]   [ŋ]   [n]   [k]
every morni**ng** and eveni**ng** and i**n** one wee**k** you'll start

      [ŋ]   [g]   [m]   [n]
seei**ng** a bi**g** difference. Your face will glea**m** and shi**n**e

      [k]   [n]
and you'll loo**k** just fi**n**e!

ANNOUNCER:
                    [m]   [m]   [n] [g]
And now for a li**m**ited ti**m**e, you ca**n** **g**et two jars for the

       [n]   [m]   [m] [n]   [m]
price of o**n**e. Re**m**ember, use Po**m**'s Ski**n** Crea**m** and

      [n]   [m]
you too ca**n** look like a fil**m** star!

ANSWERS TO SELF-TEST I ON PAGES 123–124

	2	3	1			2	3	1
1.	hot	hog	hop	6.	mad	mat	map
	3	1	2			1	3	2
2.	pat	pack	pan	7.	fade	fate	fake
	1	2	3			3	1	2
3.	save	safe	same	8.	wipe	white	wife
	3	2	1			3	2	1
4.	big	bid	bib	9.	peg	pen	pet
	1	3	2			2	1	3
5.	cake	came	cane	10.	hike	hide	height

ANSWERS TO SELF-TEST II ON PAGE 124

1. Wash your hands with _____. (soak (soap) sewn)
2. _____ the dirty dishes. ((soak) soap sewn)
3. Can you read that _____? ((sign) sight size)
4. Do the socks come in my _____? (sign sight (size))
5. I like _____ and eggs. (hat (ham) half)
6. Be home by _____ past five. (hat ham (half))
7. The _____ of the perfume is strong. (send (scent) cents)
8. A dime is worth ten _____. (send scent (cents))
9. Make a birthday _____. (whip (wish) with)
10. _____ the cream well. ((whip) wish with)

ANSWERS TO SELF-TEST III ON PAGE 125

ANN: Hi, Pam! How was your date last night with Pat?

PAM: Nothing went right last night. Pat had a flat tire and came late!

ANN: How was the food at the Old Inn?

PAM: It was bad. The soup was cold. My steak was tough. They ran out of chocolate cake.

ANN: What about the dinner Pat ate?

PAM: His duck was overdone. His garlic bread was stale!

ANN: Did it cost a lot of money?

PAM: Yes! And Pat didn't have enough to pay the bill.

ANN: I guess you won't go out with him again!

PAM: Why do you say that? We're going for a bike ride this afternoon. He's so handsome!

ANSWERS TO SELF-TEST I ON PAGES 129–130

1. We ___danced___ the rumba and tango. [t]
2. She ___talked___ on the phone for an hour. [t]
3. Dad ___painted___ the fence green. [ɪd]
4. The student ___asked___ three questions. [t]
5. They ___waited___ 15 minutes for the bus. [ɪd]
6. I've ___lived___ in the same house for four years. [d]
7. My father ___mailed___ a letter. [d]
8. The man ___walked___ five miles. [t]
9. I ___deposited___ my check in the bank. [ɪd]
10. He ___washed___ his car with a hose. [t]

ANSWERS TO SELF-TEST II ON PAGE 130

1. (stopped)   started   stated
2. (finished)   followed   phoned
3. (loved)   looked   liked
4. tasted   traded   (tapped)
5. cooked   (cleaned)   baked
6. packed   (pasted)   passed
7. ironed   sewed   (mended)
8. whispered   (shouted)   screamed
9. skipped   hopped   (lifted)
10. (pushed)   pulled   raised

ANSWERS TO SELF-TEST III ON PAGE 131

ROBERTA: Kate, have you ^[ɪd]started your diet? I hope you haven't

                       ^[d]
                       gained any weight.

KATE: I ^[d]boiled eggs and ^[t]sliced celery for lunch.

ROBERTA: Have you ^[d]exercised at all?

KATE: I ^[t]walked five miles and ^[d]jogged in the park.

ROBERTA: Have you ^[d]cleaned the house? Calories can be ^[t]worked off!

KATE: I ^[t]washed and ^[t]waxed the floors. I even ^[ɪd]painted the bathroom.

ROBERTA: Who ^[t]baked this apple pie? Who ^[t]cooked this ham?

KATE: When I ^[t]finished cleaning I was starved. I ^[d]prepared this food ^[d]for dinner.

ROBERTA: Oh, no! I'll take this food home so you won't be ^[ɪd]tempted.

                     I really ^[d]enjoyed being with you. Your diet is great!

KATE: What ^[d]happened? Somehow, I ^[t]missed out on all the fun.

ANSWERS TO SELF-TEST I ON PAGE 137

1. talks	walks	(runs)
2. dishes	(gates)	pages
3. pears	apples	(oranges)
4. eyes	(noses)	toes
5. (saves)	makes	cooks
6. newspapers	magazines	(books)
7. dogs	birds	(cats)
8. tables	chairs	(couches)
9. (dentists)	doctors	lawyers
10. lunches	beaches	(chimes)

CHARLES: Hi, James, What's new?
             [z]   [s]

JAMES: Nothing, Charles. All the guys have dates for the prom except me!
                 [z]   [z]   [s]

CHARLES: That's all right. You can take Bess's sister Nancy.
        [s]   [ɪz]

JAMES: What's she like?
        [s]

CHARLES: She measures about 5 feet 2 inches, has blue eyes, and
            [z]   [ɪz]   [z]

weighs 102 pounds. She looks like a model.
[z]   [z]   [s]

JAMES: Then she probably dislikes her studies.
                  [s]   [z]

CHARLES: That's not true. She enters law school after finals. She's on the
        [s]   [z]   [z]   [z]

Dean's List.*
[z]

JAMES: What are her hobbies? She probably hates sports!
             [z]   [s]   [s]

CHARLES: She golfs, plays tennis, and swims. She also dances very well.
       [s]   [z]   [z]   [ɪz]

JAMES: There's got to be SOMETHING wrong! She probably has no
      [z]

dates.
[s]

CHARLES: She has lots of boyfriends. In fact, let's make some changes. I'll
           [s]   [z]   [s]   [ɪz]

take Bess's sister! You can take Mary.
[ɪz]

JAMES: NO WAY! There will be no exchanges! Nancy sounds great. I
                          [ɪz]   [z]

just hope she likes me!
            [s]

ANSWERS TO SELF-TEST I ON PAGE 147

1. bead	(great)	leave	tea
2. (eight)	either	believe	niece
3. scene	(women)	these	even
4. need	(been)	sleep	thirteen
5. police	thief	machine	(vision)
6. (pretty)	wheat	sweet	cream
7. people	(bread)	deal	east
8. (tin)	teen	steam	receive
9. leave	(live)	leaf	lease
10. steep	Steve	easy	(still)

ANSWERS TO SELF-TEST I ON PAGE 149

1. ① 2   (sit   seat)
2. 1 ②   (feet   fit)
3. ① 2   (fist   feast)
4. 1 ②   (eat   it)
5. ① 2   (list   least)

ANSWERS TO SELF-TEST I ON PAGE 151

1. field   (filled)
2. (bean)   bin
3. neat   (knit)
4. deal   (dill)
5. (beat)   bit

ANSWERS TO SELF-TEST II ON PAGE 151

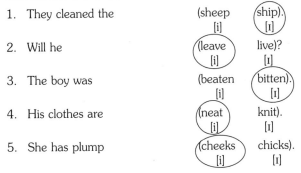

1. They cleaned the   (sheep   ship).
      [i]   [ɪ]

2. Will he   (leave   live)?
      [i]   [ɪ]

3. The boy was   (beaten   bitten).
      [i]   [ɪ]

4. His clothes are   (neat   knit).
      [i]   [ɪ]

5. She has plump   (cheeks   chicks).
      [i]   [ɪ]

ANSWERS TO SELF-TEST III ON PAGE 152

1. Take a **dip in** the **deep** water.
    [ɪ] [ɪ]   [i]
2. They **picked Tim** for the **team**.
    [ɪ]   [ɪ]   [i]
3. **Please beat** the **sweet cream**.
    [i] [i]   [i] [i]
4. **She will sit in** the **seat**.
    [i] [ɪ] [ɪ] [ɪ]   [i]
5. The **heat** wave **hit** the **city**.
    [i]   [ɪ]   [ɪ]

ANSWERS TO SELF-TEST I ON PAGE 155

(steak)	lettuce	(mayonnaise)	cereal
bread	(raisins)	melon	bananas
(cake)	(tomatoes)	(bacon)	(baking soda)
(potatoes)	crackers	peas	ice cream
(grapes)	celery	(gravy)	carrots
(toothpaste)	peas	squash	(paper plates)

ANSWERS TO SELF-TEST II ON PAGE 156

1. (practice)	plate	play	place
2. stay	aid	(plaid)	raid
3. neighbor	freight	(height)	eighty
4. (head)	great	break	came
5. shave	(any)	staple	pays
6. (America)	Asia	Spain	Maine
7. laid	crayon	(seven)	tame
8. great	grace	grey	(greedy)
9. obtain	awake	create	(breakfast)
10. snake	obey	(breath)	complain

ANSWERS TO SELF-TEST III ON PAGE 156

(Babe) Ruth was a (famous) (baseball) (player.) He was born and (raised) in an orphanage in Baltimore. He first (played) for the Boston Red Sox but was (later) (traded) to the New York Yankees. He (made) 714 home runs and (became) a (baseball) legend. He was (named) to the (Baseball) Hall of (Fame.) The last team he (played) for was the Boston (Braves.) He died in (1948.) Many (say) he was the (greatest) (player) of his (day.)

ANSWERS TO SELF-TEST I ON PAGE 160

1. C   (I)   (He went to **bad** early.)
2. C   (I)   (The opposite of east is **waste**.)
3. (C)   I   (She is my best **friend**.)
4. C   (I)   (The **pan** ran out of ink.)
5. (C)   I   (This is the **end** of the test.)

ANSWERS TO SELF-TEST II ON PAGE 161

MS. NELSON: **"Nelson Temporary Help."** Ms. Nelson speaking. Can I help you?

MR. EVANS: Yes, this is Mr. Evans. I need a temporary secretary.

MS. NELSON: What kind of secretary do you need?

MR. EVANS: The BEST! That means well educated and with excellent clerical skills.

MS. NELSON: Anything else?

MR. EVANS: Yes. I like pretty secretaries with good legs. Get what I mean?

MS. NELSON: Yes, I do. I have the best secretary for you. I'll send one Wednesday at ten.

MR. EVANS: Thanks. It's been a pleasure talking to you.

MS. NELSON: Evelyn, get me Ted Benson's file. He's an excellent secretary and has very good legs!!!

ANSWERS TO SELF-TEST I ON PAGE 164

1. (1)   2   3   (rack   rock   wreck)
2. 1   2   (3)   (lake   lock   lack)
3. (1)   2   3   (add   aid   Ed)
4. 1   (2)   3   (pot   pat   pet)
5. 1   2   (3)   (top   tape   tap)

ANSWERS TO SELF-TEST II ON PAGE 165

Dear Mom and Dad,

At last we are in San Francisco. It's a fabulous city! As we stand at the top of Telegraph Hill we can see Alcatraz. We plan to catch a cable car and visit Grant Avenue in Chinatown. After that, we'll have tea in the Japanese Gardens. Yesterday we drank wine in Napa Valley. We also passed through the National Park. Our last stop is Disneyland in Los Angeles. We'll be back next Saturday.

Love,

Gladys

P.S. We need cash. Please send money fast!

ANSWERS TO SELF-TEST I ON PAGE 168

(condor)   (collie)   leopard   (llama)
cat   tiger   (hippopotamus) (dolphin)
(fox)   (iguana)   (lobster)   (octopus)

ANSWERS TO SELF-TEST II ON PAGE 169

DONNA: (Bob,) I (want) to talk to you.

BOB: (Are) you all right?

DONNA: Don't be (alarmed.) I saw Dr. (Johnson) at the (hospital.) You're going to be a (father)!!!! Our new baby will be born on (October) 5th.

BOB: I'm in (shock.) How do you feel?

DONNA: I'm feeling "(on) (top) of the world." I've (got) a list of names for our new baby.

BOB: If it's a girl, let's call her (Donna) after her (Mom.)

DONNA: "(Donna)" is fine for a middle name. How about (Connie) or (Barbara) as her first name?

BOB: To be (honest,) I'm (fond) of the name (Barbara.) But you (forgot) that we might have a boy. How about (Bob) Junior?

DONNA: I like the name (Bob) a (lot!) How about (Tom) or (John) for his middle name?

BOB: OK, our girl will be (Barbara) (Donna) (Scott.) We can call her "(Bobbie)" for short.

DONNA: If it's a boy, his name will be (Robert) (John) (Scott) and we can still use the nickname "(Bobby.)"

BOB: (Stop) — what if we have twins?

DONNA: I'm (NOT) ready for that (problem.) (Watching) one little (tot) will be enough, (Pop!)

ANSWERS TO REVIEW TEST I ON PAGE 173

1. Leave the car in the   (shed   (shade)
                                  [ɛ]   [eɪ]

2. Do you know what was   (sad   (said)?
                                  [æ]   [ɛ]

3. We need more   (paper) pepper).
                                  [eɪ]   [ɛ]

4. Please clear that   (debt   (date).
                                  [ɛ]   [eɪ]

5. Children like   (pets   pats).
                                  [ɛ]   [æ]

ANSWERS TO REVIEW TEST II ON PAGE 174

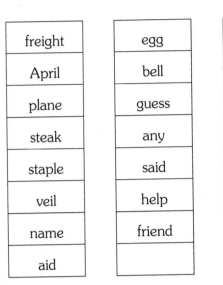
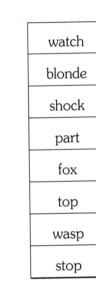

[eɪ] as in *ATE*	[ɛ] as in *EGG*	[æ] as in *HAT*	[a] as in *HOT*
freight	egg	match	watch
April	bell	vast	blonde
plane	guess	apple	shock
steak	any	half	part
staple	said	can't	fox
veil	help	laugh	top
name	friend	plaid	wasp
aid			stop

ANSWERS TO SELF-TEST I ON PAGE 178

1. 1   2   ③   (look   look   Luke)
2. 1   ②   3   (cook   kook   cook)
3. ①   2   3   (fool   fall   full)
4. ①   2   3   (mood   mud   made)
5. ①   2   3   (suit   sat   soot)
6. ①   2   3   (wooed   wade   would)
7. ①   2   3   (stewed   stood   stayed)
8. 1   ②   3   (toll   tool   tall)
9. 1   2   ③   (pull   pole   pool)
10. 1   ②   3   (skull   school   scale

ANSWERS TO SELF-TEST I ON PAGE 180

1. C (I) (You **shooed** drive carefully.)
2. (C) I (I like chocolate chip **cookies**.)
3. C (I) (He **stewed** on the ladder.)
4. C (I) (The carpenter sawed the **wooed**.)
5. C (I) (The pool was **fool** of water.)
6. (C) I (The police caught the **crook**.)
7. (C) I (The gun has **bullets**.)
8. C (I) (Please don't **pool** my hair.)
9. (C) I (I like coffee with **sugar**.)
10. (C) I (He broke his left **foot**.)

ANSWERS TO SELF-TEST I ON PAGE 182

1. 1 2 (3) (look look Luke)   6. 1 2 (3) (wooed wooed would)
2. 1 (2) 3 (cook kook cook)   7. (1) 2 3 (stewed stood stood)
3. 1 2 (3) (fool fool full)   8. 1 2 (3) (could could cooed)
4. (1) 2 3 (pull pool pool)   9. (1) 2 3 (wooed wood wood)
5. 1 2 (3) (suit suit soot)   10. (1) 2 3 (hood who'd who'd)

ANSWERS TO SELF-TEST II ON PAGE 182

Harry (Houdini) was a magician known (throughout) the world. He could (remove) himself from chains and ropes and could walk (through) walls! (Houdini) was born in (Budapest,) Hungary. He (moved) to (New) York when he was twelve and (soon) took up magic. (Rumors) spread that (Houdini) had (supernatural) powers. However, he was (truthful) and stated that his tricks could be understood by all (humans!) (Houdini) is an idol for all "would-be" magicians.

ANSWERS TO SELF-TEST I ON PAGE 188

COCKTAILS

Sake   Wine   (Rum Punch)

APPETIZERS

(Stuffed Mushrooms)   Shrimp Cocktail   Egg Roll

SOUPS

Won Ton   (French Onion)   Clam Chowder

SALADS

Hearts of Lettuce   Caesar   (Tomato and Cucumber)

VEGETABLES

(Buttered Corn)   Baked Potato   Carrots

ENTREES

Shrimp Tempura   Prime Ribs   (Roast Duck)

BREADS

Italian Bread   (Hot Muffins)   Garlic Rolls

DESSERTS

(Pumpkin Pie)   Vanilla Pudding   Ice Cream

BEVERAGES

Coffee   Milk   (Cup of Tea)

ANSWERS TO SELF-TEST II ON PAGE 189

1. Ⓒ   I   (I like toast and **butter**.)
2. C   Ⓘ   (I wish you good **lock**.)
3. C   Ⓘ   (Please **calm** to my house.)
4. Ⓒ   I   (It is hot in the **summer**.)
5. C   Ⓘ   (He **cot** the steak with a knife.)

ANSWERS TO SELF-TEST I ON PAGE 192

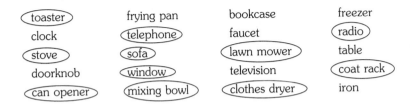

(toaster)	frying pan	bookcase	freezer
clock	(telephone)	faucet	(radio)
(stove)	(sofa)	(lawn mower)	table
doorknob	(window)	television	(coat rack)
(can opener)	(mixing bowl)	(clothes dryer)	iron

ANSWERS TO SELF-TEST II ON PAGE 193

JOE: (Rose,) let's (go) on a trip. We need to be (alone.)

ROSE: (OK,) (Joe.) Where should we (go?)

JOE: I (know!) We'll (go) to (Ohio.)

ROSE: Great! We'll visit my Uncle (Roland.)

JOE: (No,) it's too (cold) in (Ohio.) We'll (go) to (Arizona.)

ROSE: Fine. We'll stay with your Aunt (Mona!)

JOE: (No,) it's too hot in (Arizona.) Let's (go) to (Rome.)

ROSE: Oh, good! You'll meet my Cousin (Tony.)

JOE: (No,) (no,) (no!!) We (won't) (go) to (Rome.) Let's (go) to (Nome,) Alaska. We (don't) (know) anyone there!!

ROSE: You (won't) believe it, but I have an (old) friend . . .

JOE: (Hold) it, (Rose,) we (won't) (go) anywhere! I (suppose) we'll just stay (home.)

ANSWERS TO SELF-TEST I ON PAGE 197

1. ① 2 (It's in the **hall**. It's in the **hull**.)
2. 1 ② (I dropped the **bowl**. I dropped the **ball**.)
3. ① 2 (I said **talk**. I said **tuck**.)
4. 1 ② (The **stock** is high. The **stalk** is high.)
5. ① 2 (He **sawed** it. He **sewed** it.)

ANSWERS TO SELF-TEST II ON PAGE 197

AUDREY: Hi, (Paula.) Did you hear the (awful) news? (Maude) (called) (off) her wedding to (Claude!)

PAULA: Why, (Audrey?) I (thought) they were getting married in (August.)

AUDREY: (Maude) kept (stalling) and decided (Claude) was the (wrong) man.

PAULA: Poor (Claude.) He must be a (lost) soul.

AUDREY: Oh no. He's (abroad) in (Austria) having a (ball!)

PAULA: I (almost) forgot. What about the (long) (tablecloth) we (bought) them?

AUDREY: I (already) (brought) it back. The (cost) of the (cloth) will cover the (cost) of our lunch today.

PAULA: (Audrey,) you're (always) so (thoughtful!)

ANSWERS TO REVIEW TEST I ON PAGES 200–201

1.	([ʌ])	[ou]	[ɔ]	[a]	(come	fun	us)
2.	[ʌ]	[ou]	[ɔ]	([a])	(shop	watch	pot)
3.	[ʌ]	[ou]	([ɔ])	[a]	(lost	shore	fall)
4.	[ʌ]	([ou])	[ɔ]	[a]	(blown	close	sold)
5.	[ʌ]	[ou]	[ɔ]	([a])	(John	Bob	Tom)
6.	([ʌ])	[ou]	[ɔ]	[a]	(brother	uncle	cousin)
7.	[ʌ]	[ou]	([ɔ])	[a]	(cause	flaw	moth)
8.	[ʌ]	([ou])	[ɔ]	[a]	(bowl	soak	hold)
9.	[ʌ]	[ou]	([ɔ])	[a]	(cross	fault	more)
10.	([ʌ])	[ou]	[ɔ]	[a]	(Monday	Sunday	month)

ANSWERS TO REVIEW TEST II ON PAGES 201–202

$\hspace{4em}$[ʌ]$\hspace{4em}$[ʌ]
A Man *From Kentucky*

$\hspace{8em}$[ʌ]$\hspace{6em}$[ʌ]
A man from *Kentucky* named *Bud*

$\hspace{2em}$[ʌ]$\hspace{3em}$[ʌ]$\hspace{2em}$[ʌ]$\hspace{5em}$[ʌ]
Had a *lucky young son* named *Jud*

$\hspace{10em}$[ɔ]
When he bet on a *horse*

$\hspace{4em}$[ɔ]$\hspace{4em}$[ɔ]
It never *lost*, of *course*

$\hspace{2em}$[ʌ]$\hspace{7em}$[ʌ]$\hspace{5em}$[ʌ]
But *one* day it got *stuck* in the *mud*!

[a]$\hspace{2em}$[a]$\hspace{5em}$[a]$\hspace{6em}$[a]
Tom's father was a *farmer* named *Bob*

$\hspace{2em}$[a]$\hspace{6em}$[a]$\hspace{2em}$[a]
Who *got* very confused *on* the *job*

$\hspace{2em}$[ʌ]
Among his misdeeds

$\hspace{6em}$[ʌ]
Was mixing *some* seeds

$\hspace{2em}$[a]$\hspace{5em}$[ɔ]$\hspace{5em}$[a]
His *squash* tasted like *corn* on the *cob*!

ANSWERS TO SELF-TEST I ON PAGE 205

1. a l p h ⓐ b e t
2. u t ⓘ l i z e
3. d ⓔ p e n d i n g
4. p h o t ⓞ g r a p h
5. p a p ⓐ

ANSWERS TO SELF-TEST II ON PAGE 206

1. about	oven	(create)	olive
2. minute	second	seven	(leaving)
3. (attic)	attend	allow	annoy
4. (something)	support	supply	suppose
5. combine	complete	(camper)	compare
6. Canada	Georgia	Tennessee	(Wyoming)
7. lavender	maroon	(yellow)	orange
8. (strawberry)	banana	vanilla	chocolate
9. lettuce	tomato	carrot	(cucumber)
10. giraffe	zebra	(monkey)	camel

ANSWERS TO SELF-TEST I ON PAGS 208–209

1. The **girl** wore a **purple** ____skirt____ .
2. The **Germans** bake good___desserts___ .
3. At Thanksgiving we **serve** ____turkey____ .
4. People **worship** in a ____church____ .
5. I **heard** the **chirping** of the ____bird____ .
6. Another **word** for handbag is ____purse____ .
7. A **permanent** makes your hair ____curly____ .
8. I **prefer** the scent of that ____perfume____ .
9. You should **learn** your nouns and ____verbs____ .
10. A **person** collects unemployment when he is out of____work____ .

ANSWERS TO SELF-TEST I ON PAGE 211

(acre)	(enter)	curtain	dirty
(supper)	third	(backward)	(Saturday)
shirt	nurse	(weather)	(percent)

ANSWERS TO [ɝ] AND [ɚ] REVIEW TEST ON PAGE 212

The *pearl* is one of the most (*treasured*) gems. Pearls are formed inside the shells of (oysters.) The largest pearl (fisheries) are in Asia. (Cultured) pearls were developed by the Chinese in the twentieth (century.) They are (larger) than (nature's) pearls. A perfect pearl that is round and has a great (luster) is worth a lot of money. (Perhaps) a "diamond is a girl's best friend," but pearls will always win a woman's (favor!)

ANSWERS TO SELF-TEST I ON PAGE 215

1. brown	down	(flow)	frown
2. foul	(group)	shout	loud
3. (know)	how	now	cow
4. sour	hour	(tour)	our
5. (could)	count	crown	crowd
6. (thought)	plough	drought	thousand
7. ounce	out	(own)	ouch
8. flounder	(flood)	flour	pounce
9. allow	about	power	(arose)
10. noun	(consonant)	vowel	sound

ANSWERS TO SELF-TEST II ON PAGE 216

MR. BROWN: You look **(out)** of sorts. **(How)** come?

MRS. BROWN: I'm tired (out.) Didn't you hear the (loud) noise (outside) all night?

MR. BROWN: I didn't hear a (sound.) I was ("out) like a light!"

MRS. BROWN: (Our) neighbors had a big (crowd;) they were (shouting) and (howling!)

MR. BROWN: Why didn't you tell them to stop (clowning) (around?)

MRS. BROWN: I didn't want to (sound) like a (grouch.)

MR. BROWN: Next time I'll go (out.) I'm not afraid to open my (mouth!)

MRS. BROWN: I knew I could (count) on you. Here comes our noisy neighbor Mr. (Crowley,) right (now.)

MR. BROWN: That 300-(pound) ("power)(house!") Sorry dear, I have to go (downtown,) (NOW!!)

MRS. BROWN: Come back, you (coward!!!)

ANSWERS TO SELF-TEST I ON PAGE 219

1.	price	crime	(pity)	pile
2.	mind	kind	(spinning)	finding
3.	sign	high	fright	(freight)
4.	(list)	cite	aisle	cried
5.	(gyp)	bye	cry	reply
6.	(niece)	nice	knife	night
7.	style	(failed)	filed	fire
8.	(pretty)	try	resign	goodbye
9.	ice cream	eye	(aim)	aisle
10.	flight	fine	(duty)	dying

ANSWERS TO SELF-TEST II ON PAGE 220

MIKE: **(Hi,) (Myra!)** It's **(nice)** to see you.

MYRA: (Likewise,) (Mike,) How are you?

MIKE: (I'm) (tired.) (I) just came in on a (night) (flight) from (Ireland.)

MYRA: What (time) did your (flight) (arrive?)

MIKE: (I) (arrived) at (five) forty-(five) in the morning.

MYRA: (I'm) (surprised) the (airlines) have a late (night) (flight.)

MIKE: If you don't (mind,) (Myra,) (I) think (I'll) go home and rest for (awhile.) (I'm) really ("wiped) out!"

MYRA: It's (quite) all (right.) (Goodbye,) (Mike!)

ANSWERS TO SELF-TEST I ON PAGE 223

1. voice	avoid	void	(vows)
2. noise	(nose)	hoist	annoy
3. (towel)	toy	toil	spoil
4. Detroit	Illinois	St. Croix	(New York)
5. oil	oily	foil	(owl)
6. boil	broil	(bow)	boy
7. poison	(pounce)	point	appoint
8. poise	Joyce	(Joan)	soil
9. coil	(coal)	coy	coin
10. (lobster)	sirloin	oyster	moist

ANSWERS TO SELF-TEST I ON PAGE 230

1. themselves   them (selves)
2. birthday   (birth) day
3. engineer   en gi (neer)
4. September   Sep (tem) ber
5. Saturday   (Sat) ur day

ANSWERS TO SELF-TEST II ON PAGE 231

1. (agent)	annoy	allow	agree
2. upon	until	undo	(under)
3. (protect)	program	pronoun	protein
4. token	toaster	(today)	total
5. supper	sunken	suffer	(support)

ANSWERS TO SELF-TEST III ON PAGE 231

     (1) 2
1. Keep a *record* of your expenses.
     1 (2)
2. The police don't *suspect* anyone.
     1 (2)
3. The student will *present* a speech.
     (1) 2
4 The *present* was not wrapped.
     (1) 2 3
5. The *invalid* was in the hospital.

ANSWERS TO SELF-TEST IV ON PAGES 231–232

    ① ②   ① 2 ① 2
MONEY by Richard Armour

  ① 2
Workers earn it,

   ① 2
Spendthrifts burn it,

  ① 2
Bankers lend it,

  ① 2
Women spend it,

  ① 2
Forgers fake it,

  ①2
Taxes take it,

① 2
Dying leave it,

     1 ②
Heirs receive it,

① 2
Thrifty save it,

  ① 2
Misers crave it,

  ① 2
Robbers seize it,

     1 ②
Rich increase it,

  ①   2
Gamblers lose it…

I could use it!   (Reprinted by permission of BRANDEN PUBLISHING, Boston)

ANSWERS TO SELF-TEST I PAGE 237–238

1. (Mary) is a (good) (friend.)
2. (Steve) is (tall) and (handsome,)
3. It's (early) in the (morning.)
4. The (baby) (caught) a (cold.)
5. I (ate) a (piece) of (pie.)
6. The (store) (opens) at (nine.)
7. My (shoes) (hurt) my (feet.)
8. (Please) (look) for the (book.)
9. He's (leaving) in a (week.)
10. We (walked) in the (snow.)

ANSWERS TO SELF-TEST II PAGE 238

1. black **bird**	(**black**bird)
2. copper **head**	(**copper**head)
3. (blue **bell**)	**blue**bell
4. light **house**	(**light**house)
5. (white **house**)	**White** House

ANSWERS TO SELF-TEST III ON PAGES 238–239

1. Mary wants _a_ cup _of_ coffee.
2. The show started _at_ eight.
3. The movie _was_ very funny.
4. Sue ate _a_ slice _of_ cake.
5. We met _a_ couple _of_ friends _of_ mine.

ANSWERS TO SELF-TEST IV ON PAGE 239

1. Mary is Anne's (friend.) (She isn't her cousin.)
2. John is (married) to Anne. (They aren't engaged anymore.)
3. She's from Washington, (D.C.) (She's not from Washington state.)
4. She lives in the white (house.) (She doesn't live in the White House.)
5. Her house is on First (Street.) (It isn't on First Avenue.)
6. Anne and John got married (three) years ago. (Not five years ago.)
7. They (own) a small home. (They don't rent.)
8. Mary wants to come in a (week.) (She doesn't want to wait a month.)
9. She'll bring her (collie) and snakes. (She's not bringing her poodle.)
10. Mary is opening a (pet) store. (Not a toy store.)

ANSWERS TO SELF-TEST I ON PAGE 245

1. _I'm_ a student. (I am)
2. Lynn _doesn't_ play tennis. (does not)
3. _We've_ seen that movie. (We have)
4. _You're_ quite right. (You are)
5. His brother _can't_ come. (cannot)
6. He _hasn't_ arrived yet. (has not)
7. _We'll_ be ten minutes late. (We will)
8. I don't think _they're_ coming with us. (they are)
9. My son _wasn't_ there. (was not)
10. My car _isn't_ ready yet. (is not)

ANSWERS TO SELF-TEST II ON PAGE 245-246

1. <u>Meet me at the bus stop // after you're done.</u>
   Meet me at the bus // stop after you're done.

2. Bill Brown the mayor will // speak tonight.
   <u>Bill Brown // the mayor // will speak tonight.</u>

3. <u>Please clean your room // before leaving.</u>
   Please clean your // room before leaving.

4. The truth is I don't // like it.
   <u>The truth is // I don't like it.</u>

5. <u>He was there // for the first time.</u>
   He was there for // the first time.

6. <u>Charles Dickens // the famous author // wrote *David Copperfield*.</u>
   Charles Dickens the famous author wrote // *David Copperfield*.

7. <u>Where there's a will // there's a way.</u>
   Where there's a // will there's a // way.

8. Do unto others as // you would have them do // unto you.
   <u>Do unto others // as you would have them // do unto you.</u>

9. <u>Patrick Henry said // "Give me liberty // or give me death."</u>
   Patrick Henry // said "Give me // liberty or give me death."

10. When in Rome do // as the Romans do.
    <u>When in Rome // do as the Romans do.</u>

ANSWERS TO SELF-TEST I ON PAGE 252

1. (Ron did 90 sit-ups.)
2. It only cost ten cents.
3. (He's really smart.)
4. (She's been married eight times.)
5. You drank two gallons of wine.

Ron did 90 sit-ups.
(It only cost ten cents.)
He's really smart.
She's been married eight times.
(You drank two gallons of wine.)

ANSWERS TO SELF-TEST II ON PAGE 253

1. When's your birthday? ↘
2. Did you see my friend? ↗
3. How are you? ↘
4. I'm fine, thank you. ↘
5. Why were you absent? ↘
6. Can you have dinner? ↗
7. I don't like beets. ↘
8. How do you know? ↘
9. Where is the pencil? ↘
10. What is your name? ↘

ANSWERS TO SELF-TEST III ON PAGE 253

1. We enjoy swimming, → hiking, → and tennis. ↘
2. Is a barbecue all right → if it doesn't rain? ↗
3. If it rains tomorrow → the game is off. ↘
4. Is he sick? ↗ I hope not. ↘
5. Please bring me the hammer, → nails, → and scissors. ↘
6. Do you like grapes, → pears, → and plums? ↗
7. May I leave now, → or should I wait? ↘
8. He's good at math, → but not spelling. ↘
9. Call me later, → if it's not too late. ↘
10. Will you visit us → if you're in town? ↗